Proceedings of the ROW15 – Real Option Workshop

Editors: Mikael Collan and Pasi Luukka

LUT Scientific and Expertise Publications
Tutkimusraportit – Research Reports, ISSN-L 2243-3376, ISSN 2243-3376
Number 44

ISBN 978-952-265-834-0 (Printed)
ISBN 978-952-265-835-7 (PDF)

Table of Contents

Preface

This proceedings is the official publication of the ROW15 – Real Option Workshop. The topic of the workshop was "real options research in general" and the proceedings include ten double-blind peer-reviewed and presented abstracts and papers.

We wish to thank all the contributors to the workshop and especially thank the workshop keynote speakers: professors Christer Carlsson and Leonid Chechurin.

The workshop was supported by The Finnish Real Options Society (FROS), The Finnish Operations Research Society (FORS), and Lappeenranta University of Technology (LUT). The organizers thank the aforementioned for their support.

We hope that you will enjoy the workshop and wish you a pleasant stay in the city of Lappeenranta and at the Lappeenranta University of Technology.

Prof. Mikael Collan
ROW15 Local Organizing Committee Chair
ROW15 International Scientific Programme Committee Chair

Prof. Pasi Luukka
ROW15 Local Organizing Committee Co-Chair
ROW15 International Scientific Programme Committee Co-Chair

Prof. Stein-Erik Fleten
ROW International Scientific Programme Committee Co-Chair

Local organizing committee:

Mikael Collan, LUT, Finland (Chair)
Pasi Luukka, LUT, Finland (Co-chair)

International Scientific Programme Committee:

Mikael Collan, LUT, Finland, (Chair)
Stein-Erik Fleten, NTNU, Norway (Co-chair)
Pasi Luukka, LUT, Finland (Co-chair)
Mario Fedrizzi, U. Trento, Italy
Yuri Lawryshyn, U. Toronto, Canada
Christer Carlsson, Åbo Akademi, Finland
Makoto Goto, Hokudai U., Japan
Kalevi Kyläheiko, LUT, Finland
Jozsef Mezei, Åbo Akademi, Finland
Markku Heikkilä, Åbo Akademi, Finland
Tero Haahtela, Aalto U., Finland
Farhad Hassanzadeh, U. North Carolina, USA
Jani Kinnunen, Åbo Akademi, Finland
Eero Kasanen, Aalto U., Finland
Luiz Brandão, PUC-RIO, Brazil
Lauri Frank, U. Jyväskylä, Finland
Marco Antonio Guimaraes Dias, PUC-RIO, Petrobras, Brazil
Jörg Freiling, University of Bremen, Germany
Michel-Alexandre Cardin, NUS, Singapore

ROW15 Workshop Schedule

Tuesday – August 18th

10.00 Opening ceremony

10.20 Keynote I - Christer Carlsson

11.20 Lunch break

12.20 Paper Sessions I (Chair: Mikael Collan)

> 1. Linnerud and Boomsma - Revision of renewable-electricity support schemes: How policy uncertainty affects investments

> 2. Aas, Andresen, Fleten, Mazieres, and Nadarajah - Operation, Valuation and Electricity Sourcing for an Aluminum Smelter

> 3. Collan, Savolainen, and Luukka - Screening the value of a mining asset portfolio - a simulation approach

> 4. Savolainen - Valuation of metal mining assets - review

14.00 Break

14.30 Paper Sessions II (Chair: Yuri Lawryshyn)

> 1. Haahtela - Comparison of Diabetes Type 1 Treatment Total Life-time Costs: Multiple daily injection method vs. advanced hybrid closed-loop insulin pump with continuous glucose monitoring

> 2. Kostrova, Finger, and Djanibekov - Farm-Level Model of Short-Rotation Coppice Cultivation with Flexibility in Planting and Harvesting

> 3. Kozlova, Collan, and Luukka - Comparing Datar-Mathews and fuzzy pay-off approaches to real option valuation

> 4. Davison and Lawryshyn - Valuing Managerial Cash-Flow Estimates with Market Related Timing Risk

16.15 End of the first workshop day

In the evening: Conference Dinner (details will be communicated when they become available)

Wednesday – August 19th

10.00 Keynote II – Leonid Chechurin

11.00 Lunch break

12.00 Paper Sessions III (Chair: Pasi Luukka)

      1. Schwanitz - Geoengineering under uncertainty

      2. Morreale, Rose, and Lo Nigro - R&D alliances timing under uncertainty: from theory toward experiments

      3. Kinnunen and Georgescu - Real Option Values and Financial Ratios in Finnish Stock Market

13.20 Closing ceremony

Revision of renewable-electricity support schemes: How policy uncertainty affects investments

Kristin Linnerud
Centre for International Climate and
Environmental Research
NO–0318 Oslo, Norway
Email: kristin.linnerud@cicero.oslo.no
Corresponding author. Phone: +47 94873338

Trine Krogh Boomsma
University of Copenhagen
Department of Mathematical Sciences
2100 Copenhagen, Denmark
Email: trine@math.ku.dk

Abstract—Renewable-electricity support schemes are applied in almost 100 countries. Using EU as an example, we show that these support schemes can be divided in three categories: a fixed price replacing the electricity price (e.g., feed-in tariffs), a fixed subsidy on top of the stochastic electricity price (e.g., feed-in premium) or a combination of two stochastic prices (e.g., tradable green certificates). A more market-oriented scheme will result in a better working power market. Using a real options approach we show that: 1) risk difference between feed-in tariffs on one side and feed-in premium and tradable green certificates on the other is not so big, 2) an expected transition to a more market oriented scheme can result in smooth changes in investment rates in contrast to an unexpected transition, and 3) this will be the case even though the revision affects old and new installations alike.

I. INTRODUCTION

Renewable-electricity support schemes are applied in almost 100 countries. Using EU as an example, we show that these support schemes can be divided in three categories: a fixed price replacing the electricity price (e.g., feed-in tariffs), a fixed subsidy on top of the stochastic electricity price (e.g., feed-in premium) or a combination of two stochastic prices (e.g., tradable green certificates).

Depending on the design of these support schemes, the cash inflows to investment projects will be more or less exposed to fluctuations in electricity and/or subsidy prices. In addition to this market risk is the risk that the policy will change in the future. A greater influx of intermittent renewable electricity funded by fixed feed-in tariffs challenges the functioning of power markets. In a communication on the internal energy market published in November 2012, the EU Commission suggests that the support schemes are revised to better reflect market mechanisms.

II. METHOD

We examine how such market and policy uncertainties affect investment decisions in the renewable electricity sector. The benchmark case is a situation in which investors expect the current support scheme to stay the same indefinitely. We assume that investors receive an electricity price and a subsidy payment for each unit of electricity produced. We allow for different combinations of deterministic and stochastic, geometric Brownian motion diffusion processes. The resulting

models can be used to evaluate support schemes of tradable green certificates (both prices are stochastic), feed-in premiums (a stochastic electricity price and a deterministic subsidy payment) and feed-in tariffs (only a deterministic subsidy payment). We further assume that at some random point in time, the subsidy payment will be revised, and that investors either expect or do not expect that this decision will be retroactively applied. This is modeled by including a Poisson jump process.

We formulate the investment decision as a real option problem in which the option to delay an irreversible investment decision has a value (Dixit and Pindyck, 1994). Our optimization problems are solved analytically using dynamic programming. The essence of this method is to compare the value of immediate investment with the expected value of delaying the investment decision. In our case, finding the optimal timing of an investment implies identifying the sum of the electricity price and the subsidy payment—the threshold revenue—that defines the border between the continuation region (in which the optimal decision is to wait) and the stopping region (in which the optimal decision is to invest). Uncertainty will affect the value of the option to wait and therefore this threshold.

Our approach builds directly on [3] and is related to [4] and [1]. [4] examine investment timing and capacity choice under uncertainty in capital costs, electricity price and subsidy payments under different renewable electricity support schemes, and the possibility of a change from one support scheme to another. Using simulations they find that feed-in tariffs encourage earlier investments than feed-in premiums and green certificates. [1] derive the investment timing for a renewable energy facility with price and quantity uncertainty, where there might be a subsidy proportional to the quantity of production. Including the possibility that the subsidy is retroactively terminated, they conclude that a subsidy, even one having an unexpected withdrawal, will hasten investment compared to a situation with no subsidy. Like [4] we allow for more than one stochastic price process in order to realistically model the support schemes in use. We extend their analysis by allowing for correlation in prices to better investigate the risk of green certificates under different assumptions of price dependencies. In order to more clearly convey how individual price and policy uncertainties are related to the threshold revenue, we choose to derive the solution analytically following an approach developed in [2] and applied in [1]). While [1] and [3] examine the prospects of scheme termination, we extend their analysis by allowing for an expected change from one support scheme to another at an uncertain point in time.

We first derive implicit solutions to the optimization problem and then solve them numerically by fixing the electricity price and finding the solution to n equations in n unknowns. Using a windpower casestudy we illustrate the impact of policy uncertainty relative to the benchmark case where the current scheme is applied idefinitely.

III. CONCLUSION

A more market-oriented scheme will result in a better working power market. Using a real options approach we show that: 1) risk difference between feed-in tariffs on one side and feed-in premium and tradable green certificates on the other is not so big, 2) an expected transition to a more market oriented scheme can result in smooth changes in investment rates in contrast to an unexpected transition, and 3) this will be the case even though the revision affects old and new installations alike. Consequently, we advise an open political debate on how to market-orient the renewable-electricity support schemes in EU and other countries where fixed feed-in tariffs or similar schemes are in use today.

ACKNOWLEDGMENT

We thank Roger Adkins, Derek Bunn, Stein-Erik Fleten, Dean Paxson, Afzal Siddiquy, particpants at the 19th International Real Options Conference, 2015 and two anonymous referees at the Real Options Workshop, 2015 for valuable comments on earlier versions. We thankfully acknowledge support from the Research Council of Norway through project number 228811/E20 (RISKY-RES).

REFERENCES

[1] Adkins R, Paxson D. Subsidies for renewable energy facilities under uncertainty. Article published online. The Manchester School; 20 February 2015. http://dx.doi.org/10.1111/manc. 12093.

[2] Adkins R, Paxson D. Renewing assets with uncertain revenues and operating costs. Journal of Financial and Quantitative Analysis 2011; 46(3):785–813.

[3] Boomsma TK, Linnerud K. Market and policy risk under different renewable electricity support schemes. Energy 2015, http://dx.doi.org/10.1016/j.energy.2015.05.114.

[4] Boomsma TK, Meade N, Fleten S-E. Renewable energy investments under different support schemes: A real options approach. European Journal of Operational Research 2014; 220(1):225–237.

[5] Dixit AK, Pindyck RS. Investment under uncertainty. Princeton University Press; 1994.

Operation, Valuation, and Electricity Sourcing for a Generic Aluminium Smelter

Sven Henrik Andresen, Eivind F. Aas, Stein-Erik Fleten

Dept of Industrial Economics and Technology Management
Norwegian University of Science and Technology
Trondheim, Norway
svenhenrikandresen@gmail.com

Denis Mazieres
Birkbeck, University of London
London, UK

Selvaprabu Nadarajah
College of Business Administration
University of Illinois at Chicago
Chicago, Illinois, USA

Abstract— An aluminium producer is concerned with operating the smelter in a manner that maximises its value and minimises shutdown risk. Operational flexibility is available through mothballing or closure whereas procurement of electricity, a dominating input cost, may be done in the spot market or through long-term bilateral contracts. The producer faces multiple risk factors such as changes in aluminium price, electricity price and foreign exchange rates. We present a joint valuation and optimization approach for evaluating a smelter and deriving a risk minimising electricity procurement strategy. Determining an operational policy to maximize smelter value is done by using the least squares Monte Carlo (LSM) method. Electricity procurement is solved by a linear optimization program that minimises a trade-off between power cost and Conditional Value-at-Risk (CVaR). The results indicate that an aluminium producer can reduce mothballing and closure risk by determining an operating policy with the LSM and deriving a corresponding electricity procurement strategy in the form of a portfolio of spot and long-term bilateral contracts. This also reduces the expected shutdown costs incurred and thus has a positive effect on the smelter value.

Keywords—Least squares Monte Carlo; real options; portfolio optimisation; stochastic dynamic programming; electricity sourcing; Ornstein-Uhlenbeck; three-factor commodity process; ConditionalValue-at-Risk   (CVaR)

Screening the value of a mining asset portfolio - A simulation approach

M. Collan, J. Savolainen and P. Luukka

Lappeenranta University of Technology / School of Business and Management, Lappeenranta, Finland
savoljyr@gmail.com; {mikael.collan; pasi.luukka}@lut.fi

Abstract—This paper presents a simulation model for estimating the Real Option Value (ROV) of a mining asset portfolio containing different types of projects with varying risk levels instead of valuing assets separately. Characteristics of metal mining projects are discussed, the proposed method is described and its functionality is illustrated numerically with a two-project portfolio suggesting that the diversification of projects may be used for optimizing shareholder value. The value of postponing options within the given set of projects is estimated.

Keywords—*Metal Mining, Investment analysis, Real options*

I. INTRODUCTION

Metal mining investments are long lifetime capital investments with low level of reversibility. Once the key parameters of a mining system design (technical solution, capacity choice, etc.) have been decided, there may be only a limited room for feasibility improvement [1] which highlights the importance of initial analysis. The projects' economic value is dependent on the development of metal markets [2], [3].

The mining industry nowadays is dominated by a very limited number of large companies having multiple mining assets both operational and under development. The currently available real option valuation (ROV) methods can be criticized for being applicable only to single projects or isolated investment proposals and not to strategic decision making (see [4]). Evidently, the situation calls for quantitative tools to equally value not only a single, but a variety of preliminary projects, where the best information available is incomplete, and often vague or imprecise. By diversification of assets, the investor can decrease the commodity-specific risk [5], which allows to both maximize the expected return of portfolio and minimize its variance [6].

The applicability of widely recognized Brennan & Schwartz [7] –theory on mining investments company-level of on the mining investments' operating policies may be compromised when having to take into account the company specific features such the number of mining operations in the company´s portfolio of projects (see discussion in [8]). Further, in valuation of mining companies not only the operational flexibility to temporarily shut down of mines should be considered, but also the companies' options to obtain additional production through acquisition and exploration activities [3].

The inherent uncertainty of economic reserve size [9]–[11] and internal dynamics of mining investments [12], [13], the various sources of uncertainty [14] and the scarcity of information make the valuation of prospective metal mining projects difficult to perform with the most commonly used (static) investment analysis methods [15]: net present value (NPV), internal rate of return (IRR), and the pay-back method.

In scientific literature, there are examples on mining project valuations using different types of valuation frameworks: binomial trees [16]–[20], Black & Scholes [21], [22] option pricing [23], NPV [24], NPV based real option valuation (ROV) [25] among others. In a survey of 20 mining companies in 1995 [26], a discounted cash flow analysis DCF was used by 95% of respondents. The choice of analysis method is related to the project phase, type and the amount of unresolved uncertainties as the simplest methods are largely constrained by the number of variables. From practical decision making point of view, the use of multiple tools in capital budgeting will likely lead to an inability in arriving into mutually comparable values [27]. Further, the aforementioned investment analysis methods do not consider the value of flexibility (real options). Suitable real option analysis methods for under parametric uncertainty include methods using fuzzy logic to model the imprecise information available [28], [29] and simulation based models [30], [31].

The option to postpone investment is of key importance for the metal mining industry. Firstly because of the relatively irreversible nature of the investments [11] (downside risk) and, secondly, the possible value-added by optimal timing [24] (upside potential). We also add the limited resources of a company available to undertake several large projects at once. In a strategic perspective, there is obviously a commitment-flexibility trade-off on sustaining a competitive advantage by investing [4], [32], [33]. However, taking into account the non-renewable nature of primary metal resources, the changes for competitors' pre-emptive investments are limited disregarding their exploration and R&D efforts.

The correlation of cash flows with market indices in RO-valuation has been proposed in [34]. Valuing interrelated projects in real option theory framework is earlier covered in [35], who develop analytical solutions on the choice of development strategy. In a recent contribution of [36] an equity portfolio is simulated using a least squares Monte Carlo –method and different investment styles. Early stage mining projects are analyzed for example in [37]–[39]. [40] uses the portfolio terminology in valuing a multi-zoned metal reserve of a single, operating project. [41] applies simulation technique to analyze financing alternatives of a gold mine. To the best of our knowledge, there no earlier attempts to create an investment valuation model for a multi-mine asset portfolio.

By extending the ideas Datar & Mathews [31] (D-M – method), we introduce a project portfolio valuation tool for "fast and dirty" screening of mining assets controlled or available to the company. The total real option value of an asset portfolio is calculated by simply deriving it from the simulated NPV-value distributions of individual assets. The most optimal development policy can be chosen from the set of calculated ROVs of simulated policies thus reducing the subjective factors of corporate decision making. The proposed application of D-M -model overcomes two common restrictive assumptions on the analysis of early stage projects: firstly the volatilities of metal mining seldom equal to volatility of commodity prices [42] and, secondly, the forecasts of future prices do not have to be normally distributed as the historical data analysis suggest [5], [43]–[45]. These features also allow a more realistic value analysis of postponement option compared to traditionally used methods.

We hold an underlying assumption that the illustrated company wishes to stay in business by profitably exploiting both of the two analyzed reserves which have a proven or conditional techno-economic feasibility. Therefore the portfolio optimization question actually reduces to *when to optimally invest* in project rather than whether to invest or not. The operational option for temporary closure is excluded from the analysis assuming its value to be small compared to investment timing and assuming that marginal mines with high option values are rarely developed as greenfield projects (see [11], [24], [46]–[48]). Option to abandon is left outside the scope of this paper for simplicity. The proposed method assumes that the prevailing uncertainty is of parametric type [49] and the number of possible outcomes of projects is somewhat known allowing a quantitative real option analysis (see discussion [32]). The ultimate effect of diversification decisions on company's market value is not considered (see discussion [50]).

The paper is organized as follows. In the next section, we discuss the theoretical concerns of mining valuation with NPV and then introduce the underlying mechanics of applied portfolio valuation model built with Matlab® software. The approach is compared to the traditional spreadsheet functionality. Third section presents a numerical example of an illustrative mining portfolio with two projects: one greenfield copper (Cu) early-stage development project ("Mine *a*") and a brownfield nickel(Ni)-copper-gold(Au) operation ("Mine *b*"). The paper ends with discussion and propositions on future research guidelines.

II. THEORY BACKGROUND

A. NPV of a multi-metal mining operation

Our proposed method lays its foundations on the principles of DCF analysis, which provides a clear methodology for 'go' or 'no go' type decisions that the companies are faced with regarding the development of projects [47]. We assume that as the DCF formula can be applied to each project separately, it should work also for any collection of projects as well [50].

To prove the theoretical applicability of valuation approach, we first analytically estimate the value limits of

a mining project with one metal, where a finite ore reserve, $Q < \infty$, is to be mined with a constant yearly production capacity of ore P_d, during m_{tot} ($1 \leq m_{tot} \leq \infty$) years (see similar ideas for petroleum industry in [48]). The one-metal mine model is then extended to cover several metals and multiple (prospective) mining operations. The design capacity of the mine (units of metal per year) can be written as a function of reserve estimate and mine lifetime as:

$$P_d = \frac{\theta Q}{m_{tot}} \tag{1}$$

where θ represents the metal grade of ore ($0 \leq \theta \leq 1$). The designed capacity cannot exceed the physical inventory of metal: $\theta Q \geq P_d$. We denote R ($0 \leq R \leq 1$) as the recovery rate of metal in terms of physical recovery, which is limited by the ore type, metal content, and the set of feasible technical solutions, which may be unknown at the time of the analysis. The product is sold as a metal concentrate and the payment rate ρ ($0 < \rho \leq 1$) is the ratio relative to the metal market price. $C_p(P_d) > 0$ is the unit cost of production per produced ton and $C_I(P_d) > 0$ the total investment cost - both dependent on the initial capacity decision. The net present value of mine in case of immediate investment, can be written as:

$$NPV = \sum_{t=0}^{m}\left(\frac{\rho R P_d S_t}{(1+r_{rev})^t} - \frac{C_p(P_d)}{(1+r_{cost})^t}\right) - C_I(P_d) \tag{2}$$

where r_{rev} *and* r_{cost} represent the discount rates for revenues and costs, and S_m the price of metal.

If the project is delayed the investment cost $C_I(P_d)$ is discounted to the year of investment, denoted with t_0,

$$NPV = \sum_{t=0}^{m}\left(\frac{\rho R P_d S_t}{(1+r_{rev})^t} - \frac{C_p(P_d)}{(1+r_{cost})^t}\right) - \frac{C_i(P_d)}{(1+r_{cost})^{t_0}} \tag{3}$$

In an "ideal case", where 100%-purity metal ($\theta \to 1$) would be extracted from ground with no cost, then

$$R \to 1, \rho \to 1, C_p(P_d) \to 0 \text{ and } C_I(P_d) \to 0 \tag{4}$$

Combining (1), (2) and (4) we get a maximum project value for any single metal mining project exercised immediately, which would be perfectly correlated with the market price:

$$NPV = \sum_{t=0}^{m} \frac{Q S_t}{m_{tot}(1+r_{rev})^t} \tag{5}$$

In a multi-metal mine the total sum of ore contents cannot be more than 100%: i.e. $0 \leq \theta_1 + \ldots + \theta_\omega \leq 1$, where ω presents the number of metals extracted. Note that θ-values are restricted by the geological properties of the reserve and they cannot be changed arbitrarily. By substituting P_d in (5) with (1), the maximum revenue is the discounted total value of all metal elements present in the ore can be written as:

$$NPV = \sum_{z=1}^{\omega}\sum_{t=0}^{m} \frac{Q(\theta_z S_{z,t}+\cdots+\theta_\omega S_{\omega,t})}{m_{tot}(1+r_{rev})^t} \tag{6}$$

5

Disregarding upside potential of price uncertainty, the maximum value of (6) is achieved by immediate extraction as t → 0 (and $m_{tot} = 1$).

In an "ideal negative case", where an investor has a non-extractable (but possible very large reserve), or the products are unsellable, then

$$R \to 0, \text{ or } \rho \to 0 \qquad (7)$$

By combining (2) and (6) and denoting actual production with P_a, the NPV becomes the sum of the costs:

$$NPV_{min} = \sum_{t=0}^{m} -\frac{C_p(P_a)}{(1+r_{cost})^t} - C_I(P_d) \qquad (8)$$

If the ore is discovered to be non-extractable, the extreme (theoretical) downside case is

$$P_a \to 0, \text{ and } m_{tot} \to \infty, \text{ thus } NPV_{min} = -\infty \qquad (8)$$

The realizable value of a multi-metal mining project in the planning phase is,

$$-\infty \leq NPV \leq Q(\theta_1 S_{1,0} + \cdots + \theta_\omega S_{\omega,0}) \qquad (9)$$

In a case of multi-mine portfolio having a number of φ mines with ω different metals in each, the total portfolio maximum value is the sum of maximum values of individual mines,

$$-\infty \leq NPV_{tot} \leq Q^1(\theta_1^1 S_{1,0}^1 + \cdots + \theta_\omega^1 S_{\omega,0}^1) + \cdots + Q^\varphi(\theta_1^\varphi S_{1,0}^\varphi + \cdots + \theta_\omega^\varphi S_{\omega,0}^\varphi) \qquad (10)$$

To derive a non-ideal form for multi-mine value we use equation (3) and a common industry practice of writing the production costs as a function of the metal which generates the majority of revenues (z = 1) in multi-metal mines. The extended form of equation (3) can be written as

$$NPV = \sum_{z=1}^{\omega} \sum_{t=0}^{m} \left(\frac{P_d(S_{z,t}\rho_z R_z + \cdots + S_{\omega,t}\rho_\omega R_\omega)}{(1+r_{rev})^t} - \frac{C_p(P_d)}{(1+r_{cost})^t} \right) - \frac{C_I(P_d)}{(1+r_{cost})^{t_0}} \qquad (11)$$

In a portfolio of multi-metal mines the equation (11) is expanded to cover multiple mines (1 to φ) similarly as written in the maximum value equation (10).

The theoretical infinite negative value of a portfolio is not relevant in practice, because of the inherent option to abandon. In reality, an investor has to optimize the value of portfolio on the basis of a finite set of available technical solutions by maximizing the expected ore tonnages (P_d), product qualities (ρ) and metal recoveries (R) and minimizing the total costs of extraction (C_p, C_I) in the planning stage of individual mines (P_a is not known).

$$max \, NPV(max[P_d^1], max \sum_{z=1}^{\omega} ([R_z^1, \rho_z^1] \dots [R_\omega^1, \rho_\omega^1]),$$

$$min[C_p^1(P_d^1), C_I^1(P_d^1)] + \cdots$$
$$+ max \, NPV(max[P_d^\varphi], max \sum_{z=1}^{\omega} ([R_z^\varphi, \rho_z^\varphi] \dots [R_\omega^\varphi, \rho_\omega^\varphi]),$$
$$min[C_p^\varphi(P_d^\varphi), C_I^\varphi(P_d^\varphi)]) \qquad (12)$$

Assuming organizational limitations and stochastic prices, the investor has to decide which projects should be implemented, postponed or abandoned to create the optimal expected total pay-off distribution in terms of maximum NPV and minimum variance. Note that also θ (i.e. cut-off grade) can be optimized in both strategic planning and mining operation. However, because the increase of cut-off grade leads to discarding of some parts of the physical reserve, the optimal decision may be either to minimize or maximize cut-off grade depending on the metal price, plant capacity and available operational strategies such as stockpiling possibilities (see discussion in [1], [12], [51]–[55]). Because the preliminary nature of analysis, we leave the cut-off grade considerations out of this paper. We highlight the fact that including the θ-optimization into early stage analysis will also lead to re-iterations of reserve size Q and probably higher order forms of NPV-equations.

The analysis method proposed is aimed at providing support in presenting the range of outcomes stylized in (3), when extended to cover multi-mine portfolio (see (11)) under the uncertainty of the metal price (S_t) and some of the projects' parameters (equation (12)).

B. Proposed Method

The proposed method is based on a set of Matlab-scripts that are run in series. We denote the total timeframe of the simulation as t_{tot}, the production time period as t_{prod}, and the time before production start-up as $t_{no-prod}$. The total number of simulation rounds is n. Illustration of the simulation method is visible in Figure 1.

The procedure can be divided into the following phases:

i) Creation of discount rate vectors for costs and revenues for the analysis timeframe, t_{tot}. In general, revenue discount rates depend on the projects' risk level, but the cost discount rate is held constant for all projects (company's cost of money). Using separate discount rates for costs and revenues is discussed, e.g., in [30]. The cost and revenue discount vectors are replicated n times to create intermediate matrices of the dimension [$t_{tot} * n$];

ii) Initialization of probability distribution objects of uncertainties in analyzed projects. The probability distributions are specified by the user, and they are modeled according to a selected distribution type (shape) and value limits;

iii) Generation of n random paths for market uncertainties (e.g., metal price(s) and inflation) for the total timeframe of the analysis (in this case 40 years). The result is a matrix with dimension [$t_{tot} * n$] for each random path dependent uncertainty;

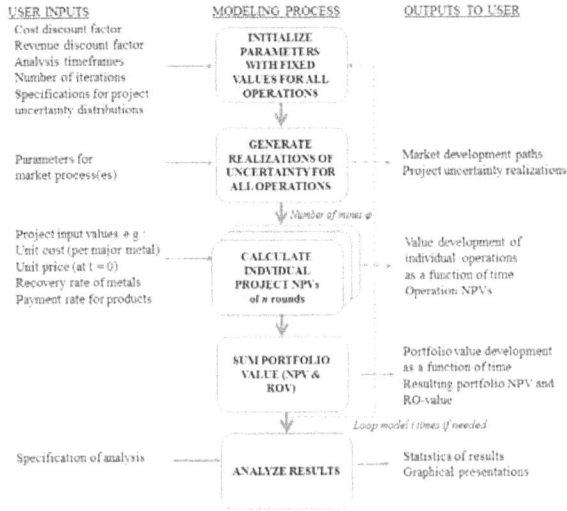

Figure 1. A general illustration of the proposed method for valuing a portfolio of prospective mining projects

iv) n random draws from the defined probability distributions for each uncertain "project parameter". Each drawn value is fixed for the simulation period and the resulting matrix size for each project uncertainty is [1 * n]. The matrices are replicated as needed, e.g., the production unit cost matrix is multiplied by the yearly production rates and grows to in dimension to [t_{prod} * n];

v) Concatenating matrices into a size [t_{tot}, n] for NPV-calculation purposes. For example, the total cost matrix is created by concatenating (1) a matrix of exploration cost [1 * n] for year zero, (2) a possible zero-matrix for delay time [$t_{no-prod}$ * n], (3) a matrix of the investment cost [1 * n], (4) matrix of production costs [t_{prod} * n], and (5) a zero-matrix of the period after reserve depletion [(t_{tot}- $t_{no-prod}$- t_{prod}) * n];

vi) NPV-calculation using the concatenated matrices. For example, the n possible yearly revenues for each mine is calculated as: "production schedule matrix" multiplied with the "price path matrix" and divided with the "revenue discount matrix";

vii) Summing up NPV-calculation results from step (vi) i.e. portfolio value. The RO-value is calculated by taking into account the probability of negative outcomes of resulting distributions (see [30]). Descriptive numbers from the results are generated including mean values, quintiles, variances, cumulative sums, and generation of graphs.

One of the main results of an analysis is a histogram resulting from $\varphi*n$ NPV values (n = 100000 and φ = 2 in our example). The histogram is a net present value distribution for the set of prospective metal mining projects. For additional analysis of single variables, e.g., the effect of changes in delay times to the profitability of the project, it is possible to loop the model steps from i to vi a desired number of times.

The method utilizes the strengths that the used MatLab (short for matrix laboratory) software offers with regards to matrix calculations and is therefore able to perform faster than by using the said software in running similar analysis via an iterative process.

III. NUMERICAL ILLUSTRATION

A. Illustrative Case Description

We assume a mining company with two assets. The first asset (Mine a) is a promising undeveloped reserve, where the type of ore and its metal contents in terms of % or g/ton are known. The second asset (Mine b) is an abandoned, end of life multi-metal mine (copper, gold and nickel) with a 10 years lifetime and an existing mining infrastructure requiring an 800 M$ financial investment for the change of ownership and operations re-start.

The Mine a example is modified from [56]. The exact size of undeveloped Cu-reserve is unknown and an additional exploration investment is required. We assume that the exploration investment of 20 M$ or 40M$ is always made in the start of the simulation (t = 0), because it is relatively small compared to total investment size and it greatly reduces the prevailing uncertainty. Table 1 shows the expected results of exploration investment and its resulting investment for the actual mine. We assume that the mining operation will be planned with a 20 year lifetime as follows: if reserve = 1.0 Mtn, the yearly production will be 50 000 ton Cu/year (1 000 000 tons / 20 years) and 100 000 ton Cu/year if reserve equals 2.0 Mtn respectively. In a case of empty reserve, the production will be zero and no investment is made.

TABLE I

EXPECTED COPPER RESERVE AND RESULTING INVESTMENT SIZE IN MINE B.

MINE A: Developed Reserve (proven)

Metal	Reserve	Investment		Prod. rate
	Mtn	$M		tn/year
Ni, Mtn	0.25		->	25 000
Au, tons	50	800$M	->	5
Cu, Mtn	0.125		->	12 500

MINE B: Undeveloped Reserve (conditional to exploration)

Reserve Cu, Mtn	Probability %	Investment $M		Prod. Rate tn/year
0,0	25	0	->	0
1,0	25	350	->	50 000
2,0	50	450	->	100 000

To simplify the analysis, we assume that the recovery (95%) and payment rate (95%) of metals for both reserves are known with certainty. We acknowledge the values are way above average industry values, but we disregard the issue here, as it has no effect on the mechanics of the proposed method. Production costs have some uncertainty, which are modeled as triangular distributions. On the basis of contingency of returns, the revenue discount for mine a is set to 8% and 5% for mine b. The company-wide discount rate is set to 3%. The key variables of the two projects are summarized in table 2.

7

TABLE II

KEY VALUES OF THE TWO PROJECTS AND MODEL ASSUMPTIONS

Project variable	Min	Value	Max	Unit
Unit Cost				
Mine A (± 25%)	1 860	2 480	3 100	$/ton Cu
Mine B (± 5%)	11 400	12 000	12 600	$/ton Ni
Revenue discount				
Mine A	-	8,0	-	%
Mine B	-	5,0	-	%
Cost Discount	-	3,0	-	%
Payment rate	-	95	-	% of metal
Recovery	-	95	-	% of metal

B. Analysis Results

In the simulation we use assumptions of 1) uncorrelated, 2) perfectly negatively correlated and 3) perfectly positively correlated price processes. For simplicity, the effect of correlation is analyzed only between copper to other metals (Ni and Au) even though multiple other alternatives do exist. The underlying geometric Brownian motion (GBM) parameters are visible in table 3. Without going to price modeling in detail, we simply assume here that the price trends are based on subjective managerial estimates: copper price level does not change, but the nickel and gold price have an increasing price trend.

TABLE III

ASSUMPTIONS FOR STOCHASTIC METAL PRICE PROCESSES

Market variable	Value	Unit
Copper price, t_0	6 362	$/ton
Nickel price, t_0	13 825	$/ton
Gold price, t_0	39	$/g
Cu return	0,0	%/year
Cu volatility	5,0	%/year
Ni return	2,5	%/year
Ni volatility	10,0	%/year
Au return	5,0	%/year
Au volatility	3,0	%/year

To simulate perfect price correlations we create n price paths for copper and calculate their yearly returns. If the prices are (positively/negatively) correlated, then the return for correlated metal (Au or Ni) is:

$$[Au/Ni\ change] = ±[Cu\ change]*[Au/Ni\ vol.]/[Cu\ vol.] + [Au/Ni\ return] \quad (2)$$

For example, assuming perfect negative price correlation and a price change of copper for +3%. Then following equation (2) for the respective Ni-price change is -1.5% (i.e. -3*10/5+2.5) and for gold-price 3.2% (-3*3/5+5). Following the simulation process in figure 1. We start by running the simulation model with uncorrelated prices for 100000 times and the results are illustrated as histograms in figure 2 and 3.

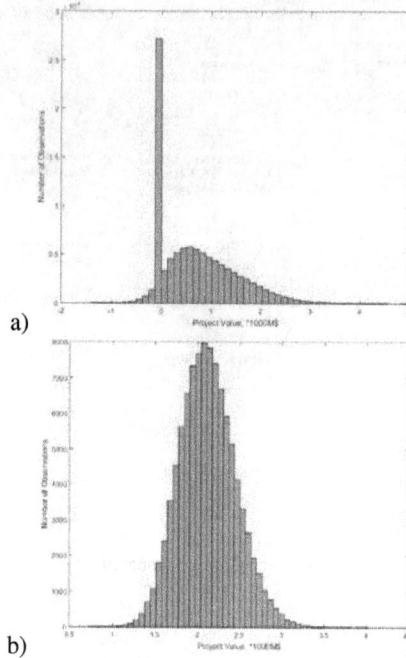

a)

b)

Figure 2. Example histograms of individual project values using uncorrelated prices: a) Mine *a* (Cu), b) Mine *b* (Ni, Cu, Au)

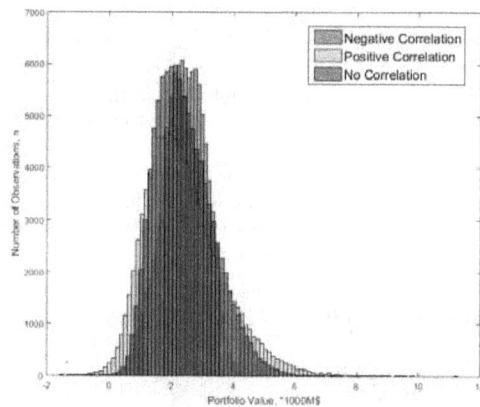

Figure 3. Example of portfolio value histograms (Mine *a* + Mine *b*) using different price assumptions.

The histogram in figure 3 indicates that the variation of results increases with positive correlation and decreases with negative correlation of prices. Note, that the projects are always correlated to some extent as the copper is produced from both reserves.

To further refine the analysis, the investment riskiness of possible investment policies may be evaluated on the basis of variance or standard deviation and the number of negative results (table 4). The interesting feature in results with GBM-price process modeling is that the portfolio's mean value is very little affected by the correlation. This is probably largely due to fixed price trends of Ni- and Au-return assumptions which create a large part of the total portfolio value. The real option values are close to expected NPVs, because of low probability of negative outcomes in all the simulated cases. To calculate the real option value of an investment (portfolio) we use the following equation [30]:

$$ROV = (1-[Probability\ of\ negative\ outcomes])\ *$$
$$[Expected\ value\ of\ the\ positive\ values] \qquad (13)$$

TABLE IV
PORTFOLIO VALUE WITH DIFFERENT PRICE CORRELATION ASSUMPTIONS

Price correlation	NPV Mean	Standard dev.	Neg. NPV	ROV
(Cu to Ni and Au)	M$	% of mean	outcomes	M$
No correlation	2412,4	39,2	13	2412,1
Positively correlated	2401,2	51,3	498	2389,2
Negatively correlated	2399,4	28,8	1	2399,4

We can conclude that in an ideal situation, the choice of development would be simply to go ahead with both projects. However, in reality the investment policy decision making is likely to be constrained by several "in-house" factors such as the availability of capital, availability of key personnel able to start-up complex operations, political uncertainties of countries where the reserves are located, company's risk preferences, etc. Postponing option is possibly the easiest and most often available method to address these limitations. Therefore, we assume having a ~10 year strategic planning horizon, which gives 81 (9x9) possible combinations of delaying projects. In figure 4 is shown the calculated mean values of possible portfolio values, when delay option is applied to projects *a* or *b*.

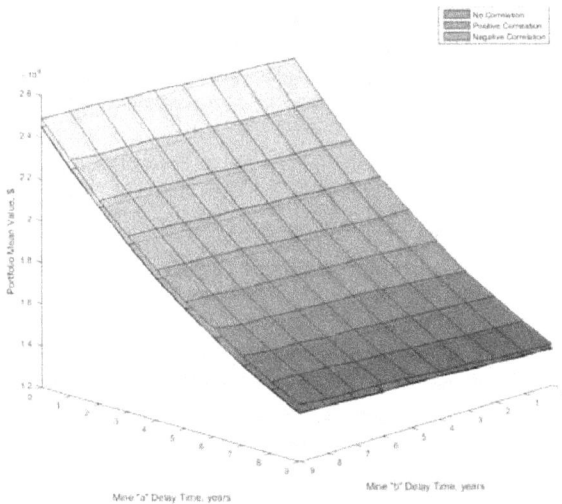

Figure 4. Average mean value of asset portfolio as a function of time using different correlation assumptions of metal prices. Observe that delay times on axis x and y are from increasing to decreasing.

With the given market forecasts (positive outlook on gold and nickel) it seems that the asset portfolio value would be maximized by undertaking the risky Cu-project *a* first and postponing the project *b*, which has a lower risk and therefore smaller revenue discount rate in our model. The decision making suggestion to invest on a less profitable project contradicts with the intuition of implementing the most profitable projects first. The result should not be over interpreted, as the more detailed price modeling can reverse the situation.

Figure 5 and 6 show that the portfolio with negatively correlated metal prices has the smallest standard deviation

in value even though the actual investment would be postponed into future. Now we apply the equation (13) to display the set of real option values of possible development strategies with delay option under consideration (figure 7).

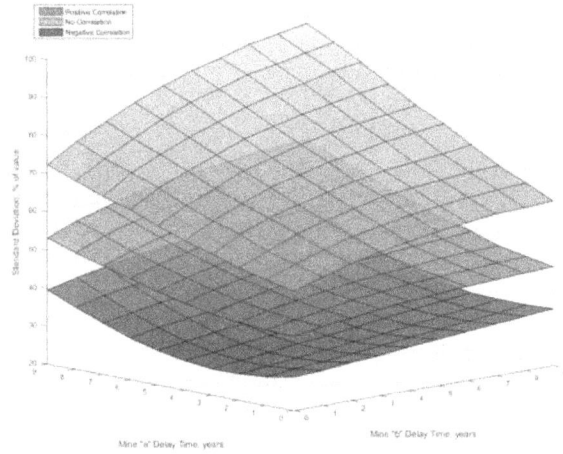

Figure 5. Standard deviation of mean values as a function of projects delay times with different price correlation assumptions.

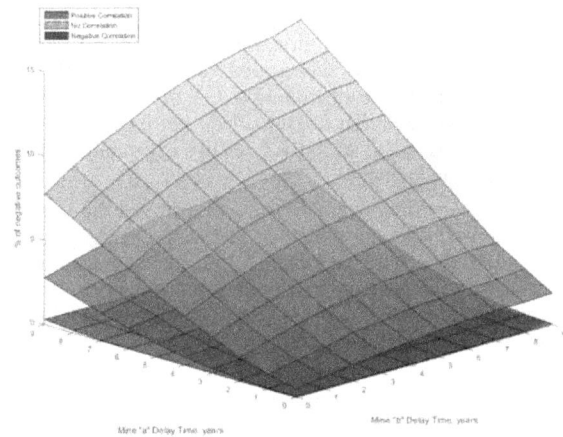

Figure 6. Amount of negative results in simulation as a function of project delay times with different price correlation assumptions.

Graphics in figure 7 indicate that the real option value of asset portfolio is the highest if market prices are mutually uncorrelated and the risk of losing value by delaying mine *b* is relatively low. On the contrary, assuming positive correlation the effect of delay option may have a significant effect on the future cash flows. The utilization of resulting analysis is dependent on the preferences of the decision maker and company policies: the portfolio can be optimized, for example in terms of maximum return on investment (~the highest resulting NPV) or the minimum volatility (i.e. standard deviation of value).

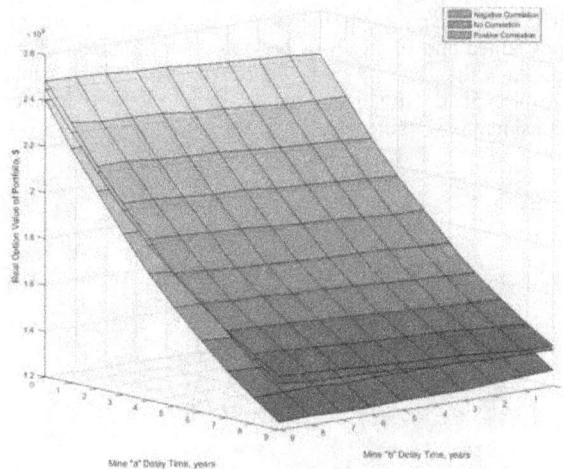

Figure 7. Average real option value of asset portfolio as a function of delay times using different correlation assumptions of metal prices. Observe that delay times on axis x and y are from increasing to decreasing.

IV. CONCLUSIONS

Using the features of Matlab® and Matlab Financial Toolbox®, we showed that several mining assets can be merged into one portfolio valuation model to calculate their combined value under multiple project and market uncertainties. In the numerical illustration we used the simplest possible case of a two asset portfolio, but the proposed method has no limitation on the number of assets. The approach extends the current scientific literature to analyzing a portfolio of mining assets instead of valuing them individually. The results can be presented with illustrative graphics, which are readily interpreted by the company management.

In our numerical example we demonstrated the models applicability with the simplest GBM-type price process. This contradicts with the fact that the actual non-renewable natural resource markets demonstrate mean reverting characteristics in the long term, which probably undermine project values indicated here (see discussion [11], [38], [48], [57]).

Regarding the applicability of model, we highlight the the ability to predict future metal price trends to some extent. However, the state-of-the-art methods on forecasting metal market prices were left for future research efforts as the focus of this paper was on the methodological aspects of valuation model. We did not address the alternative investment strategies of the two available assets such as implementing project *a* only in the cases where the realized reserve size was the largest alternative. The simulation tool presented would allow a more detailed analysis on the resulting value distributions for competing alternatives as discussed previously in, e.g., [58]–[60]. Also the possibilities of reducing investment risk via joint-ventures were not considered here. The development decision in terms of plant capacity could be also defined as a function of price [48] and the planned cut-off grade θ could be altered with discrete steps depending on forecasted market conditions. These issues should be addressed in the future research.

ACKNOWLEDGMENT

Authors wish to thank Finnish Cultural Foundation, Kainuu Regional fund for funding this research

REFERENCES

[1]   B. Hall, "How mining companies improve share price by destroying shareholder value," in *Proceedings CIM Mining Conference and Exhibition*, 2003, pp. 1–17.

[2]   D. G. Baur, "Gold mining companies and the price of gold," *Rev. Financ. Econ.*, Aug. 2014.

[3]   P. Tufano, "The Determinants of Stock Price Exposure: Financial Engineering and the Gold Mining Industry," *J. Finance*, vol. 53, no. 3, pp. 1015–1052, Jun. 1998.

[4]   T. Driouchi and D. J. Bennett, "Real Options in Management and Organizational Strategy: A Review of Decision-making and Performance Implications," *Int. J. Manag. Rev.*, vol. 14, no. 1, pp. 39–62, 2012.

[5]   M. H. Chen, "Understanding world metals prices-Returns, volatility and diversification," *Resour. Policy*, vol. 35, no. 3, pp. 127–140, 2010.

[6]   H. Markowitz, "Portfolio selection," *J. Finance*, vol. 7, no. 1, pp. 77–91, 1952.

[7]   M. J. Brennan and E. S. Schwartz, "Evaluating Natural Resource Investments," *J. Bus.*, vol. 58, no. 2, pp. 135–157, 1985.

[8]   A. Moel and P. Tufano, "When Are Real Options Exercised? An Empirical Study of Mine Closings," *Rev. Financ. Stud.*, vol. 15, no. 1, pp. 35–64, 2002.

[9]   G. W. Evatt, M. O. Soltan, and P. V. Johnson, "Mineral reserves under price uncertainty," *Resour. Policy*, vol. 37, no. 3, pp. 340–345, Sep. 2012.

[10]   A. D. Akbari, M. Osanloo, and M. A. Shirazi, "Reserve estimation of an open pit mine under price uncertainty by real option approach," *Min. Sci. Technol.*, vol. 19, no. 6, pp. 709–717, Nov. 2009.

[11]   M. Slade, "Valuing managerial flexibility: An application of real-option theory to mining investments," *J. Environ. Econ. Manage.*, vol. 41, pp. 193–233, 2001.

[12]   Y. Azimi, M. Osanloo, and A. Esfahanipour, "An uncertainty based multi-criteria ranking system for open pit mining cut-off grade strategy selection," *Resour. Policy*, vol. 38, no. 2, pp. 212–223, Jun. 2013.

[13]   A. M. Newman and M. Kuchta, "Using aggregation to optimize long-term production planning at an underground mine," *Eur. J. Oper. Res.*, vol. 176, no. 2, pp. 1205–1218, 2007.

[14]   Z. Mayer and V. Kazakidis, "Decision making in flexible mine production system design using real options," *J. Constr. Eng. Manag.*, no. February, pp. 169–181, 2007.

[15]   P. A. Ryan and G. P. Ryan, "Capital Budgeting Practices of the Fortune 1000: How Have Things Changed?," *J. Bus. Manag.*, vol. 8, no. 4, p. 15, 2002.

[16]   B. Kamrad and R. Ernst, "An Economic Model for Evaluating Mining and Manufacturing Ventures with Output Yield Uncertainty," *Operations Research*, vol. 49, no. 5. pp. 690–699, 2001.

[17]   H. Dehghani and M. Ataee-pour, "Determination of the effect of operating cost uncertainty on mining project evaluation," *Resour. Policy*, vol. 37, no. 1, pp. 109–117, 2012.

[18] H. Dehghani, M. Ataee-pour, and A. Esfahanipour, "Evaluation of the mining projects under economic uncertainties using multidimensional binomial tree," *Resour. Policy*, vol. 39, no. 1, pp. 124–133, 2014.

[19] K. Sunnevåg, "An option pricing approach to exploration licensing strategy," *Resour. Policy*, vol. 24, no. 1, pp. 25–38, 1998.

[20] S. Shafiee, E. Topal, and M. Nehring, "Adjusted Real Option Valuation to Maximise Mining Project Value – A Case Study Using Century Mine," 2009.

[21] F. Black and M. Scholes, "The Pricing of Options and Corporate Liabilities," *J. Polit. Econ.*, vol. 81, no. 3, pp. 637–654, 1973.

[22] J. Huang, N. Tan, and M. Zhong, "Incorporating Overconfidence into Real Option Decision-Making Model of Metal Mineral Resources Mining Project," *Discret. Dyn. Nat. Soc.*, p. 11, 2014.

[23] M. A. Haque, E. Topal, and E. Lilford, "A numerical study for a mining project using real options valuation under commodity price uncertainty," *Resour. Policy*, vol. 39, pp. 115–123, Mar. 2014.

[24] F. Auger and J. I. Guzmán, "How rational are investment decisions in the copper industry?," *Resour. Policy*, vol. 35, no. 4, pp. 292–300, Dec. 2010.

[25] M. Samis, G. A. Davis, D. Laughton, and R. Poulin, "Valuing uncertain asset cash flows when there are no options: A real options approach," *Resour. Policy*, vol. 30, no. 4, pp. 285–298, Dec. 2006.

[26] R. R. Bhappu and J. Guzman, "Mineral Investment Decision Making: Study of Practices," *Engineering & Mining Journal*, vol. July. pp. 36–38, 1995.

[27] A. Borison, "Real Options Analysis: Where Are the Emperor's Clothes?," *J. Appl. Corp. Financ.*, vol. 17, no. 2, pp. 17–31, Mar. 2005.

[28] M. Collan, R. Fullér, and J. Mezei, "A Fuzzy Pay-off Method for Real Option Valuation," *J. Appl. Math. Decis. Sci.*, vol. 2009, pp. 1–14, 2009.

[29] D. Kuchta, "Fuzzy capital budgeting," *Fuzzy Sets Syst.*, vol. 111, pp. 367–385, 2000.

[30] S. Mathews and V. Datar, "A Practical Method for Valuing Real Options: The Boeing Approach," *Appl. Corp. Financ.*, vol. 19, no. 2, pp. 95–104, 2007.

[31] V. Datar and S. Mathews, "European real options: An intuitive algorithm for the Black-Scholes formula," *J. Appl. Financ.*, vol. 14, pp. 7–13, 2004.

[32] R. Adner and D. A. Levinthal, "What is not a Real Option: Identifying Boundaries for the Application of Real Options to Business Strategy," *Acad. Manag. Rev.*, vol. 29, pp. 74–85, 2004.

[33] W. C. Kester, "Today's Options for Tomorrows Growth," in *Real Options and Investment under Uncertainty*, E. S. Schwartz and L. Trigeorgis, Eds. The MIT Press, 2004, pp. 33–45.

[34] K. Barton and Y. Lawryshyn, "Integrating Real Options with Managerial Cash Flow Estimates," *Eng. Econ.*, vol. 56, no. 3, pp. 254–273, Jul. 2011.

[35] P. D. Childs, S. H. Ott, and A. J. Triantis, "Capital Budgeting for Interrelated Projects : A Real Options Approach," *J. Financ. Quant. Anal.*, vol. 33, no. 3, pp. 305–334, 1998.

[36] C. Bao, G. Lee, and Z. Zhu, "A Simulation-based Portfolio Optimization Approach with Least Squares Learning," in *Proceedings of the World Congress on Engineering 2014 Vol II, WCE 2014, July 2 - 4, 2014*, 2014, vol. II, pp. 0–5.

[37] L. Trigeorgis, "The Nature of Option Interactions and the Valuation of Investments with Multiple Real Options," *J. Financ. Quant. Anal.*, vol. 28, no. 1, pp. 1–20, 1993.

[38] A. E. Tsekrekos, M. B. Shackleton, and R. Wojakowski, "Evaluating Natural Resource Investments under Different Model Dynamics: Managerial Insights," *Eur. Financ. Manag.*, vol. 18, no. 4, pp. 543–575, Sep. 2012.

[39] G. Cortazar, M. Gravet, and J. Urzua, "The valuation of multidimensional American real options using the LSM simulation method," *Comput. Oper. Res.*, vol. 35, no. 1, pp. 113–129, Jan. 2008.

[40] M. R. Samis, D. Laughton, and R. Poulin, "Valuing a Multi-Zone Mine as a Real Asset Portfolio - A Modern Asset Pricing (Real Options) Approach," *Work. Pap.*, 2001.

[41] M. Samis and G. A. Davis, "Using Monte Carlo simulation with DCF and real options risk pricing techniques to analyse a mine financing proposal," *Int. J. Financ. Eng. Risk Manag.*, vol. 1, no. 3, pp. 264–281, 2014.

[42] G. A. Costa Lima and S. B. Suslick, "Estimating the volatility of mining projects considering price and operating cost uncertainties," *Resour. Policy*, vol. 31, no. 2, pp. 86–94, Jun. 2006.

[43] M. C. Roberts, "Duration and characteristics of metal price cycles," *Resour. Policy*, vol. 34, no. 3, pp. 87–102, 2009.

[44] W. C. Labys, A. Achouch, and M. Terraza, "Metal prices and the business cycle," *Resour. Policy*, vol. 25, pp. 229–238, 1999.

[45] K. T. McClain, H. B. Humphreys, and A. Boscan, "Measuring risk in the mining sector with ARCH models with important observations on sample size," *J. Empir. Financ.*, vol. 3, pp. 369–391, 1996.

[46] P. Bjerksund and S. Ekern, "Managing Investment Opportunities under Price Uncertainty: From 'Last Chance' to 'Wait and See' Strategies," *Financ. Manag.*, vol. 19, no. 3, pp. 65–83, 1990.

[47] D. Humphreys, "Comment. New approaches to valuation: a mining company perspective," *Resour. Policy*, vol. 22, pp. 75–77, 1996.

[48] M. A. Guimarães Dias, "Valuation of exploration and production assets: An overview of real options models," *J. Pet. Sci. Eng.*, vol. 44, no. 1–2, pp. 93–114, 2004.

[49] K. Kyläheiko, "Making sense of technology: Towards a synthesis between neoclassical and evolutionary approaches," *Int. J. Prod. Econ.*, vol. 56–57, pp. 319–332, 1998.

[50] S. C. Myers, "Finance Theory and Financial Strategy," in *Real Options and Investment under Uncertainty*, E. S. Schwartz and L. Trigeorgis, Eds. The MIT Press, 2004, pp. 19–32.

[51] M. W. A. Asad, "Optimum cut-off grade policy for open pit mining operations through net present value algorithm considering metal price and cost escalation," *Eng. Comput.*, vol. 24, no. 7, pp. 723–736, Oct. 2007.

[52] M. Thompson and D. Barr, "Cut-off grade: A real options analysis," *Resour. Policy*, vol. 42, pp. 83–92, Dec. 2014.

[53] R. D. Cairns and T. Shinkuma, "The choice of the cutoff grade in mining," *Resour. Policy*, vol. 29, no. 3–4, pp. 75–81, Sep. 2003.

[54] A. Bascetin and A. Nieto, "Determination of optimal cut-off grade policy to optimize NPV using a new approach with optimization factor," *J. South. African Inst. Min. Metall.*, vol. 107, no. 2, pp. 87–94, 2007.

[55] M. Waqar Ali Asad and R. Dimitrakopoulos, "Optimal production scale of open pit mining operations with uncertain

metal supply and long-term stockpiles," *Resour. Policy*, vol. 37, no. 1, pp. 81–89, 2012.

[56] S. Frimpong and J. M. Whiting, "Derivative mine valuation: strategic investment decisions in competitive markets," *Resour. Policy*, vol. 23, no. 4, pp. 163–171, 1997.

[57] K. Zhang, A. Nieto, and A. N. Kleit, "The real option value of mining operations using mean-reverting commodity prices," *Miner. Econ.*, vol. July 2014, no. DOI 10.1007/s13563–014–0048–6, Jul. 2014.

[58] M. Collan, *The Pay-Off Method: Re-Inventing Investment Analysis*, 23 June 20. Charleston, SC, 2012.

[59] M. Collan and J. Kinnunen, "A Procedure for the Rapid Pre-acquisition Screening of Target Companies Using the Pay-off Method for Real," *J. Real Options Strateg.*, vol. 4, no. 1, pp. 117–141, 2011.

[60] M. Collan and M. Heikkilä, "Enhancing Patent Valuation with the Pay-off Method," *J. Intellect. Prop. Rights*, vol. 16, no. September, pp. 377–384, 2011.

Valuation of metal mining assets

A review

Jyrki Savolainen

School of Business and Management,
Lappeenranta University of Technology
Skinnarilankatu 34, 53851 Lappeenranta, Finland
savoljyr@gmail.com

Abstract— **This paper is a state-of-the-art review on the numerical investment analysis methods used and usable in metal mining industry. We distinct two valuation paradigms: first the financial option pricing and, secondly, the traditional Net Present Value (NPV), which both use the terminology of real options. On the basis of literature review, a synthesis of existing valuation approaches is created and their applicability to different types of projects is discussed. It is suggested that the methods used are not mutually exclusive, but the choice of investment analysis and real option theory framework should be done on the basis of development phase of the project.**

Keywords—Metal Mining, Investment analysis, Real options

I. INTRODUCTION

Mining investments are capital intensive and practically irreversible projects with finite lifetimes. The long economic life, dependence on market prices of metals and multiple uncertainties of projects underline the importance of investment analysis as a tool to confirm their economic viability. The aim of study is to review state-of-the-art analysis methods used and usable in the mining industry and attempt to clarify the theoretical framework of real options in mining investment valuation. We see a gap on research on conceptualizing the suitability of analysis methods using real options theory in the context of metal mining project timeline.

We distinct two approaches for mining investment valuation, which both use the terminology of real options, but have a rather different theoretical foundations. First, the *option pricing* valuation based approach, where futures and options are used to estimate market risks and second, the conventional *Net Present Value (NPV)* approach for estimating project-specific risks and decision making flexibilities [1]–[3]. Both option pricing and NPV paradigms can be incorporated with real option (RO) framework.

We suggest that in the context of mining investments real options should be understood in two different meanings: firstly, as an application of option pricing theory to capital budgeting [4] i.e. real options *"on projects"* and secondly real options *"in projects"*. Using a definition of real options "on projects", we view the mining project as a whole consisting of a sequence of options. Options "in projects" in our view means adjusting the underlying (mining) system in response to the resolution of

uncertainties [5]. In other words, we use real options "in" projects to refer to "an industrial engineering/production management perspective [6]". The idea is presented in figure 1. The investments in mining can be made at any moment of the project's timeline. We propose that the valuation choice should be made on a case-by-case basis taking into account the project's development phase.

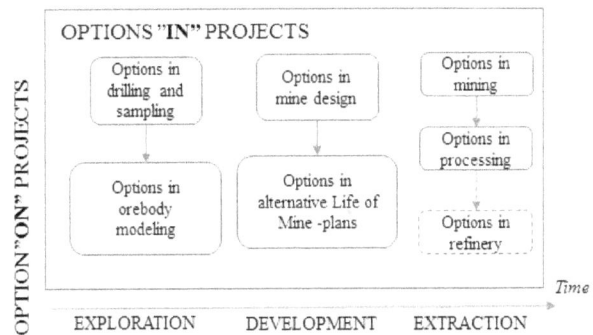

Fig. 1. Illustration of real options framework in mining industry.

This paper consists of three parts. In the following section, a literature review of investment analysis methods is conducted and its results summarized after introducing general characteristics of mining projects and their related real options. In the third section as a synthesis of existing literature, we propose a model for selecting the appropriate investment analysis method. The paper closes with conclusion and discussion.

II. LITERATURE REVIEW

A. General considerations and limitations of the review

We see the mining investment analysis as a "mature" topic with a vast accumulated knowledge. Therefore, we will concentrate on synthesizing the existing literature. From our review, we exclude some of the existing general level mining valuation methods, which are introduced in a review of Eves [7].

B. Common features of metal mining projects

The characteristics of metal mining projects have apparent similarities to oil industry investments (see [8]–[13] for petroleum project examples). Valuation of early stage projects with undeveloped reserves is complex, because of varying risks, uncertainties and asset volatility [14]. On the other hand, in a case of developed reserve, with a given mineral deposit and existing infrastructure, the major system parameters (production rate, technology, etc.) are decided and a potential for efficiency and productivity improvement may be limited [15], [16].

Relevant real options of mining operations can be identified as option to *defer* (also referred as *timing*), option to *expand*, option to *learn* and option to *abandon* (see [12]). We also add the option to *alter design* and option to *stage building* of an investment. In the context of mining industry, however, we found no references on the switch use option. There are also two mining industry specific real options: the ability to alter *cut-off grade* of mined ore and *stockpiling* of ore. Cut-off grade specifies the metal content of rock (usually % or g/tn), which is used as a material feed for the processing plant (sometimes referred also as *head grade)*. Stockpiling option means the ability to utilize waste rock stockpiles as a material feed for the processing plant in the future (see discussion in [17]).

C. Financial option theory –analysis

The work of Brennan & Schwartz [18], based on Black & Scholes [19] pricing theory on financial options, is widely recognized as the first theoretical paper on the real options in valuing mining assets [20]–[23]. They [18] formulate a general time and operation state dependent (open-close-abandon) valuation formula for operating mines. The most fundamental issue with the concept of using financial option theory for valuing real assets is usually the lack of replicating portfolio and the usual assumption of GBM-type price process [1]. As a summary, the Brennan & Schwartz model has been found to be a good stylized representation of plant-level decisions, but its usefulness may be limited to a general guidelines of strategy. The company-level applicability is restricted by the theory's inability to take into account the company specific features and the number of mining operations in the company's portfolio of projects (see discussion in [24]).

D. Net Present Value –analysis

The probably most commonly used project valuation technique in the industry discounted cash flow (DCF) methods such as NPV- and Internal Rate of Return (IRR) -analysis [25]. Essentially most decisions faced by the mining companies are "go/no go" -type choices where market valuations play no role [26]. The "dynamic cash flow models" with managerial flexibility can be distinguished from "traditional cash flow models" based on how the uncertainty of individual cash flow is dealt with in the valuation [24], [27]. The central promise of real options theory is that under uncertainty having flexible strategies

and ability to delay decisions can add value compared to making all strategic decisions during project planning [28].

A list of studies which base on the traditional NPV theory with real options is provided.

E. Bridging the gap between analysis methodologies

[2] and [3] develop an integrated approach. The dependency between market and private risk is captured by conditioning the project specific expected values for the risk-free discount rate of market risks [2].

F. Summary of literature

In the full paper, we present a concept matrix of applied methods to summarize the covered literature.

III. SYNTHESIS OF LITERATURE – A PROPOSED MODEL FOR CHOOSING THE INVESTMENT ANALYSIS METHOD

Based on the literature review, there is no single valuation paradigm generally applied to mining industry investments. We suggest that the valuation methods review should be used as complementary approaches and the selection of mining valuation method should be based on the project phase, type and its degree of uncertainty. The valuation framework is illustrated in the full paper.

In the early acquisition or exploration phase of a mining project, the uncertainty regarding reserve is the greatest. Therefore the size of the assumed cash flow can be assumed to be proportional to the market prices of extracted metal(s), but the actual cash flow size and structure is unknown. As the amount of knowledge is increased during development, the structural reserve uncertainty is unveiled setting preliminary limits for metal reserve and cash flows. When the rough costs of extraction can be estimated, it may be justified to use discounted cash flow –based methods. The value with different mine designs can be calculated to aid the decision making process. Project's feasibility is determined not only by the market performance of commodities, but also as a function of (preliminary) mining system performance including its design options to respond uncertainties. However, in the greenfield investment cases, the capital intensity of projects and limited decision horizon of managers may constraint the applicability of production design options (*in* project) postponing these into future.

The decision to invest can be seen as a turning point for decision making type: from this point on the options valued are more options *in* project than the options *on* project. By investing, one gives up the waiting option on seeing how the prices evolve in the future [29]. Reserve related parametric uncertainty is not resolved by waiting, but only through investment (see [30]).

Analysis of developed reserves

We distinct investments on developed reserves as a class of its own. We assume here, that the existing mining infrastructure and its related accumulated knowledge is to be exploited. In this, the probably most common industry case, there is no structural uncertainty of generated cash flows, in terms of magnitude and timing. NPV-based value estimates including managerial flexibility options can be derived for decision making purposes and system flexibilities (real options *in* project) may be added.

In full paper, the reviewed literature is placed on the proposed analysis framework.

IV. SUMMARY AND DISCUSSION

A literature view was conducted on the valuation paradigms and methods of metal mining investment analysis. We found no uniform basis for valuations and suggested that the valuation method should be chosen on a case-by-case basis, where project phase, uncertainty level and type of investment are taken into account. Financial option based techniques give insights to early stage projects, where the system design of a future mine is an open-ended question. Alternatively, they can be used to evaluate already developed projects in a merger-acquisition (M&A) – situations.

Theoretically undeveloped reserves have the greatest value creation potential, because of their inherent uncertainties and degrees of freedom available. This also makes their valuation the hardest and the value adding features from real options *in* project may go unnoticed as there are (structural) uncertainties to be resolved. We see that from the investment analysis point of view, recently started projects (developed reserves) may have the most degrees of freedom in choosing the valuation method. These projects have some of the technical uncertainties resolved, but they have many of the real options *in* project available for additional value creation. In our view, the decision making – theory based option valuations with NPV *in* projects have a definite applicability in cases, where the already owned operations are developed. In these cases, the market valuation is seldom needed to decide whether to implement (go/no go-) decisions.

The review suggests that there may be room for qualitative real option analysis (ROA) literature with a managerial focus on economic analysis of mining investments as the vast majority of papers included in the review concentrated on solving the numerical values of presented case examples.

ACKNOWLEDGMENT

Thanks to two anonymous reviewers in ROW15 – Real Option Workshop (18.-19.8.2015. – Lappeenranta, Finland) for their suggestions and providing some concluding remarks for the paper. This research has been supported by the Finnish Foundation for Economic Education (Suomen Liikesivistysrahasto).

REFERENCES

[1] A. Borison, "Real Options Analysis: Where Are the Emperor's Clothes?," *J. Appl. Corp. Financ.*, vol. 17, no. 2, pp. 17–31, Mar. 2005.

[2] J. E. Smith and K. F. McCardle, "Options in the Real World: Lessons Learned in Evaluating Oil and Gas Investments," *Oper. Res.*, vol. 47, no. 1, pp. 1–15, Feb. 1999.

[3] J. E. Smith and R. F. Nau, "Valuing Risky Projects: Option Pricing Theory and Decision Analysis," *Manage. Sci.*, vol. 41, no. 5, pp. 795–816, May 1995.

[4] S. P. Feinstein and D. M. Lander, "A Better Understanding of Why NPV Undervalues Managerial Flexibility," *Eng. Econ.*, vol. 47, no. 4, pp. 418–435, 2002.

[5] B. Groeneveld and E. Topal, "Flexible open-pit mine design under uncertainty," *J. Min.*, vol. 47, no. 2, pp. 212–226, 2011.

[6] J. Bengtsson, "Manufacturing flexibility and real options: A review," *Int. J. Prod. Econ.*, vol. 74, no. 1–3, pp. 213–224, 2001.

[7] C. Eves, "The valuation of long life mines: Current issues and methodologies," 2013.

[8] K. Sunnevåg, "An option pricing approach to exploration licensing strategy," *Resour. Policy*, vol. 24, no. 1, pp. 25–38, 1998.

[9] G. Cortazar, E. S. Schwartz, and J. Casassus, "Optimal exploration investments under price and geological-technical uncertainty: a real options model," *R D Manag.*, vol. 31, no. 2, pp. 181–189, Apr. 2001.

[10] J. L. Paddock, D. R. Siegel, and J. L. Smith, "Option valuation of claims on real assets: the case of offshore petroleum leases," *Q. J. Econ.*, vol. 103, no. 3, pp. 479–508, 1988.

[11] H. T. J. Smit, "Investment Analysis of Offshore Concessions in the Netherlands," *Financ. Manag.*, vol. 26, no. 2, p. 5, 1997.

[12] M. A. Guimarães Dias, "Valuation of exploration and production assets: An overview of real options models," *J. Pet. Sci. Eng.*, vol. 44, no. 1–2, pp. 93–114, 2004.

[13] M. Armstrong, A. Galli, W. Bailey, and B. Couët, "Incorporating technical uncertainty in real option valuation of oil projects," *J. Pet. Sci. Eng.*, vol. 44, no. 1–2, pp. 67–82, 2004.

[14] H. S. B. Herath and C. S. Park, "Multi-Stage Capital Investment Opportunities as Compound Real Options," *Eng. Econ.*, vol. 47, no. 1, pp. 1–27, 2002.

[15] B. Hall, "How mining companies improve share price by destroying shareholder value," in *Proceedings CIM Mining Conference and Exhibition*, 2003, pp. 1–17.

[16] L. A. Martinez and J. McKibben, "Understanding Real Options in Perspective Mine Project Valuation : A Simple abstract discounted cash flow analysis for mine project valuation," in *Minin 2010*, 2010, pp. 223–234.

[17] M. W. a Asad and E. Topal, "Net present value maximization model for optimum cut-off grade policy of open pit mining operations," *J. South. African Inst. Min. Metall.*, vol. 111, no. 11, pp. 741–750, 2011.

[18] M. J. Brennan and E. S. Schwartz, "Evaluating Natural Resource Investments," *J. Bus.*, vol. 58, no. 2, pp. 135–157, 1985.

[19] F. Black and M. Scholes, "The Pricing of Options and Corporate Liabilities," *J. Polit. Econ.*, vol. 81, no. 3, pp. 637–654, 1973.

[20] Y. Azimi, M. Osanloo, and A. Esfahanipour, "An uncertainty based multi-criteria ranking system for open pit mining cut-off grade

strategy selection," *Resour. Policy*, vol. 38, no. 2, pp. 212–223, Jun. 2013.

[21]   D. Coldwell, T. Henker, J. Ho, and K. Fong, "Real Options Valuation of Australian Gold Mines and Mining Companies," *J. Altern. Investments*, vol. 6, no. 1, pp. 23–38, 2003.

[22]   G. Cortazar, M. Gravet, and J. Urzua, "The valuation of multidimensional American real options using the LSM simulation method," *Comput. Oper. Res.*, vol. 35, no. 1, pp. 113–129, Jan. 2008.

[23]   M. A. Haque, E. Topal, and E. Lilford, "A numerical study for a mining project using real options valuation under commodity price uncertainty," *Resour. Policy*, vol. 39, pp. 115–123, Mar. 2014.

[24]   A. Moel and P. Tufano, "When Are Real Options Exercised? An Empirical Study of Mine Closings," *Rev. Financ. Stud.*, vol. 15, no. 1, pp. 35–64, 2002.

[25]   R. R. Bhappu and J. Guzman, "Mineral Investment Decision Making: Study of Practices," *Engineering & Mining Journal*, vol. July. pp. 36–38, 1995.

[26]   D. Humphreys, "Comment. New approaches to valuation: a mining company perspective," *Resour. Policy*, vol. 22, pp. 75–77, 1996.

[27]   M. Samis, G. A. Davis, D. Laughton, and R. Poulin, "Valuing uncertain asset cash flows when there are no options: A real options approach," *Resour. Policy*, vol. 30, no. 4, pp. 285–298, Dec. 2006.

[28]   S. Johnson, T. Taylor, and D. Ford, "Using system dynamics to extend real options use: insights from the oil & gas industry," *Int. Syst. Dyn. …*, pp. 1–31, 2006.

[29]   S. Majd and R. S. Pindyck, "The Learning Curve and Optimal Production under Uncertainty," *RAND J. Econ.*, vol. 20, no. 3, p. 331, 1989.

[30]   R. D. Cairns, "The Microeconomics of Mineral Extraction Under Capacity Constraints," *Nonrenewable Resour.*, vol. 7, no. 3, pp. 233–244, 1998.

Comparison of Diabetes Type 1 Treatment Total Lifetime Costs:

Multiple daily injection method vs. advanced hybrid closed-loop insulin pump with continuous glucose monitoring

Tero Haahtela

Dept. of Industrial Engineering and Management
Aalto University
Espoo, Finland
tero.haahtela@aalto.fi

Abstract—**This paper compares the costs of treating diabetes type 1 (T1D) with the commonly used multiple daily injection MDI method and with the novel method of combining insulin pump and continuous glucose monitoring (CSII + CGM) into a hybrid closed-loop system. Both direct and indirect costs of T1D treatment are considered. The lifetime costs are modeled with simulation and using discounted cash flow method. Daily basic treatment costs are twice as high with CSII+CGM in comparison with the MDI method. However, overall lifetime costs are approximately only one third of those in comparison with the MDI method. This is due to expensive indirect complication costs related to insufficient therapeutic control of many diabetics using MDI, while advanced CSII+CGM hybrid closed-loop users can avoid these complications nearly completely. At the same time, quality of life of type 1 diabetics improves significantly when using advanced CSII+CGM systems.**

Keywords—cashflow simulation, lifetime total cost estimation, uncertainty modeling, valuation, diabetes type 1 treatment cost modeling

I. INTRODUCTION

Diabetes costs represent a significant worry to both patients and the health care system. The estimated total economic cost of diagnosed diabetes in USA in 2012 was $245 billion, of which type 1 diabetes costs are $15 billion [1]. In Finland, the medical costs of treating diabetes together with the lost labor inputs of diabetic patients reduces long-run GDP by over one percent [2]. There are more than 50 000 T1D people in Finland and close to one million type one diabetics in the USA [3].

Type 1 diabetes (T1D), also called juvenile diabetes, is an autoimmune disease in which a person's pancreas stops producing insulin, a hormone that enables people to get energy from food. It occurs when the body's own immune system attacks and destroys the insulin-producing cells in the pancreas, called beta cells. T1D people need to treat themselves constantly with insulin. This is typically taken with subcutaneous injections using either insulin pens or insulin pump. Unlike with most cases of type 2 diabetes, the cause of the T1D disease is still unknown, and it is not either preventable. However, genetics and environmental triggers are

expected to be involved in the development of the disease. Diabetes and AIDS/HIV are the only two diseases that UN has officially decided to fight against.

Treatment of diabetes has improved significantly over the years. The costs are still, however, very high per person. At the moment, treatment of a diabetes type 1 patient over his lifetime costs approximately 1 million euros, of which complication costs and work absence costs are even 80 - 90 % of the total costs, and the daily basic treatment costs are 10 – 20 % [4]. Interest towards the cost structure of T1D treatment in Finland can be explained by its highest occurrence per capita in the World. In Finland, T1D rate is 58 persons per 100 000, in Scandinavia on the average the rate is 35 persons, in the USA 24, but only 1 to 100 000 in China and Japan [3].

Most typical way of treating type 1 diabetes (T1D) is to use multiple daily injections (MDI) of insulin. The method is also called flexible insulin therapy (FIT), as it gives more flexibility in treatment and life style in comparison with the conventional approach used commonly until early 1990's. Another way to treat T1D is continuous subcutaneous insulin infusion (CSII) that means using an insulin pump. This CSII method can be also enhanced with continuous glucose monitoring (CGM) where blood glucose level is continuously monitored with a sensor. In Finland, Use of CSII and CSII + CGM are considered for adults, adolescents and children with high average blood glucose levels despite of intensive MDI treatment or with occasional dangerously low blood glucose level episodes difficult to manage [5]. According to the THL research, daily basic treatment direct costs of multiple daily injection (MDI) method, excluding health care visits, are 1800 euros, with insulin pump (CSII) 3500 euros, and with insulin pump and continuous glucose monitoring (CSII + CGM), 6200 euros [5].

There are many diabetics who would like to treat themselves with the CSII or even CSII+CGM. However, some physicians deny this treatment method as they consider it to be too expensive in comparison with the expected benefits in therapeutic control and quality of life. This is also dependent of the hospital district and their policies. On the other hand, there are many physicians who consider that the expected lifetime cost with CSII and CSII+CGM would actually reduce the T1D overall costs, especially the complication costs, because of the better therapeutic control.

The purpose of this study was to compare what are the expected overall lifetime costs for treating a T1D patient with MDI/FIT or CSII+CGM methods. The analysis considers both the daily treatment costs as well as long-term complication costs of these approaches. No limitations were given in choosing the optimal valuation strategy and method. Net present value calculation, simulation, real option analysis and system dynamics were those alternatives considered mostly for finding a solution.

The structure of the paper is as follows. After the introduction, section 2 describes the complexities and risks of diabetes treatment. Section 3 discusses different diabetes treatment methods with their advantages and disadvantages. Section 4 discusses the relationship between the quality of treatment and costs of T1D. Section 5 introduces the principles of the simulation model used in lifetime cost estimation. Section 6 discusses the results of the study. Section 7 applies real option analysis qualitatively to explain why pharmaceutical companies use these options in a way that enhances the development and market competition in the field. Finally section 8 concludes the paper.

II. RISKS IN DIABETES TREATMENT

There are three different risks related to diabetes treatment: 1) hypoglycemia i.e. two low sugar level, 2) acute hyperglycemia (acute high blood glucose level with ketoacidosis), and 3) chronic hyperglycemia (high average blood glucose level) [6].

Hypoglycemia, low blood sugar, means abnormally diminished content of glucose in the blood. This is usually caused by having too much insulin in body in comparison with eaten carbohydrates and physical exercise. Effects of hypoglycemia can range from mild dysphoria to more serious issues such as seizures, unconsciousness, and (rarely) permanent brain damage or even death. As a result, people who are afraid of hypoglycemia or have a tendency for this often keep the average blood sugar on a higher level.

Hyperglycemia, high blood sugar, can be either acute of chronic. In acute hyperglycemia, a condition called ketoacidosis may develop when the body does not have enough insulin. Without insulin, the body isn't able to utilize the glucose for fuel, so the body starts to break down fats for energy. However, because there is no insulin available, this only further increases blood sugar level. Ketoacidosis is a life-threatening condition which needs immediate treatment. Symptoms of ketoacidosis are nausea and vomiting, shortness of breath, abdominal pain and dry mouth. When diabetes treatment is under control, this should not happen, especially to any adult. Most common reasons for ketoacidosis are insulin pump (cannula) obstruction, stomach diseases and purposeful neglecting the correct treatment and not dosing insulin for example due to mental stress and diabetes fatigue.

Chronic hyperglycemia means that diabetic has on average too high blood glucose rate. This average long term glucose level is also the problem that causes the diabetes complications. Blood sugar glucose connects to haemoglobin, and the higher the average blood sugar, the higher the number of sugared – glycosylated – complexes of haemoglobin and sugar. This glucose–haemoglobin complex is called glycosylated haemoglobin, otherwise known as HbA1c. This measurement tells how many (%) of the haemoglobin is sugared. Once blood cells become glycosylated, they stay glycosylated until they die (about 3 months). The new red blood cells produced are not glycosylated, but over their lifespan, may become such as a result of glucose in blood.

The typical target level set for Hba1c for adults is currently 6.5% and for children 7.5% [6]. Higher target for children is because maintaining good sugar control is trickier, as a number of factors can put them at higher risk of hypoglycemia: variable food intake, physical exercise, hormonal changes, varying rates of growth and development, and changes in emotions.

The problem with the high average blood sugar level, HaA1c, is that over time it causes most of the diabetes complications: retinopathy, kidney problems, nerve problems, foot ulcers and vascular diseases [6]. Most of these problems are caused by the sugared haemoglobin that effects negatively microvasculars. Eye and vision problems are related to retinopathy, causing trouble seeing especially at night, or in worst cases, vision loss that in many cases cannot be reversed. Another common issue is related to the kidney damages. The kidneys might not function and may even stop working, and then dialysis or a kidney transplant is needed. In Finland, diabetes is the most common reason for dialysis [7]. Nerves in the body can become damaged, causing pain, tingling, and loss of feeling. Also feet and skin can develop sores and infections, and in worst cases, part of the leg (e.g. toes) need to be amputated. Infection can also cause pain and itching in other areas. Higher blood glucose level, especially together with high blood pressure and cholesterol, can lead to heart attack, stroke, and other problems. It can become harder for blood to flow to the legs and feet.

The problems are not limited to long-term complications. Any time blood glucose levels rise particularly high, even temporarily, quality of life suffers. Short term hyperglycemia negatively affects thinking performance, coordination, emotions and moods. However, these issues do not have direct cost impacts, and therefore they were omitted in this study.

As a result, treatment of T1D is about balancing between the short-term risk of hypoglycemia and the long term risk of high blood sugar. Trying to keep HbA1c lower increases risk of hypoglycemia while playing fully safe increases risk of long-term negative side effects.

III. TREATMENT OF DIABETES: FROM CONVENTIONAL TREATMENT TO MDI AND ARTIFICIAL PANCREASES

T1D treatment has developed significantly over the last 20 - 30 years. Thirty years ago, most typical (and nearly only, and then best available) treatment for T1D was something that is now called conventional insulin therapy. Insulin was commonly dosed twice or three times a day, and meals were scheduled to match the peaks in the insulin profiles. The blood glucose level was not measured at home, and therefore the overall blood glucose levels and also the target levels were set higher than today. Nevertheless, cases of hypoglycemia were also quite common. People used to have higher HbA1c, and as a result, those who have had T1D for several decades commonly suffer to some degree of the earlier mentioned long term complications.

The next step from that was what is called multiple daily injections (MDI) or flexible insulin therapy (FIT). This approach favors flexible meal times with variable carbohydrate as well as flexible physical activities. The MDI/FIT approach became possible when new insulin analogs were developed and glucose home measuring became more accurate. These insulin analogs are very similar to real human insulin, but their amino acid sequences are genetically engineered so that they are absorbed either faster or a slower than the human insulin. As a result, they are different by their absorption, distribution, metabolism, and excretion characteristics. Usually, one or two long acting doses are taken daily, and then 4 – 6 doses of fast acting insulin analog for meals with rapid onset and shorter duration of action.

Type 1 people with MDI/FIT approach need to make frequent (5 – 8 times a day) finger sticks to check blood sugars, and also several injections of insulin. For dosing the insulin for each meal, T1D patients 1) need to measure the blood glucose, 2) calculate the number of carbohydrates of the meal and 3) take into account earlier and forthcoming physical exercise. Stress, infections, weather temperature changes and many other things also make the blood sugar level volatile (usually to increase from the ordinary level). Therefore, even the currently used MDI/FIT approach requires constant adjusting and taking carefully into account the daily routines. The advantage of MDI/FIT is the flexibility it offers to patient. The likelihood of hypoglycemia is smaller than with conventional approach, and also the HbA1c levels become better. Daily routines of MDI/FIT take a little more time than conventional therapy, but life becomes much more flexible.

The next step after MDI/FIT was the development of insulin pumps (yet the first insulin pumps were released already in the early 1980's). Insulin pump is a mobile phone sized electric device that gives user-adjusted doses of insulin. It is parameterized according to the user needs for given carbohydrates and blood glucose level. The pump then automatically suggests the optimal insulin dose for each meal. It also takes care of the basal dose that is pumped continuously at an adjustable basal rate to deliver insulin needed between meals and at night. Insulin is dosed to the body with a cannula. Current insulin pump models in 2015 also communicate wirelessly with some glucose meters and continuous glucose monitoring sensors.

Continuous glucose monitoring (CGM) is a system in which the sensor continuously reads the blood sugar level and then sends this information wirelessly either to a specific monitoring device or to the insulin pump. It is even possible to share this data with a mobile connection to the cloud in real time. The development of CGM has been rapid. In the beginning of 2010's, the sensors lasted officially only for 3 days, were not very accurate, had more size, and their insertion was not that convenient. However, in just a few years, manufacturers (e.g. Dexcom and Medtronic) have increased sensor lifespan into one or even two weeks while at the same improving their accuracy and ease of use.

As a result of this increased accuracy, latest insulin pump models can be set to act smart and lower the insulin dosing if there is a risk that user's blood glucose level goes too low. The forthcoming models - already under clinical tests [8] and scheduled to arrive in two or three years - are expected to allow also automatic insulin dosing if the glucose level goes too high.

The next step in this treatment is the so called close-loop. In this forth-coming approach, the smart device will take much more responsibility of the treatment. The closed-loop means that the device itself adjusts the basal rate and also partly fine-tunes the meal boluses. This will become possible as the CGM becomes more reliable and also faster insulin analogs can be used with the pumps. The early clinical results have shown promising results, reducing both the HbA1c and the risk of hypoglycemia. In future, also dual-hormone closed-loop approaches are under investigation, for example, using amylin analog that is normally released from pancreas along with insulin after a meal [9]. This delays glucose absorption, thus improving post-meal glucose control.

IV. TREATMENT RESULTS AND THEIR RELATIONSHIP WITH COSTS

In Finland, approximately 90 % of diabetes costs (including both type 1 and type 2) are indirect costs of complications and costs of missed work contribution and premature retirement [4]. Most common long-term complications are kidney problems (nephropathy), vision problems (retinopathy), neuropathy (nerve problems) and cardiovascular diseases. For example, depending on the source, the annual costs of dialysis treatment of kidney failure are anywhere between €50 000 to €70 000 annually. The situation has not changed since, because the average therapeutic control has not improved.

Until 1920's there was no treatment to T1D and it caused certain death very shortly. Also after that, despite of the discovery and production of insulin, life expectancy for Type 1 diabetics used to be 20 – 30 years less than for those not having diabetes. However, those born after 1965 and having diabetes Type I have life expectancy already grown to 69 [10]. According to the latest results, T1D on average reduces expected life 11 years for men and 13 for women [11]. As a result, when T1D is treated properly, nearly everyone should be able to work until the official age of retirement. To remind, there are also people who do not take care of the treatment, and might therefore die abnormally young of hypoglycemia, thus reducing the average age.

Strict control of blood sugar appears to be a key for the good treatment, life expectancy and also quality of life: researchers observed already in famous Diabetes Control and Complications Trial in 1993 that, on average, a 40% reduction in overall risk of death for every 10 reduction in patient's HbAc1 [12]. In Finland, average HbA1c in 2010 was 8.5%, very close to the earlier results of 8.6% from 1993 [13]. Yet unpublished results of 2014 suggest that current HbA1c average is 8.4%, above the current target value of 6.5 % set by Finnish Diabetes Foundation [6]. Given the technical development of the methods over the last two decades and the relatively strong public health care, this number is quite disappointing.

Alongside the complication costs, T1D causes significant losses due to early retirement related to complication costs. There are no exact numbers on this in Finland (there is no separation between type 1 and type 2), but these indirect costs are internationally considered to be significant: a bad complication may cut work life too early, and diabetic becomes a pensioner instead of being a working taxpayer. T1D may also hit personally the income of the diabetic. In the USA, T1D patient (over 18 years of age) has on average annual salary loss of $7000, and the average household income is $9500 less [14].

V.   THE CASHFOW SIMULATION MODEL

Total lifetime costs of FIT and hybrid closed-loop system treatment were modeled and compared with a discounted cash flow simulation model. The costs were grouped in two categories: daily basic treatment costs and long-term complication costs. Some daily basic treatment costs are very similar in both cases: both require insulin and blood glucose testing strips. Closed-loop system requires less insulin, and due to continuous glucose monitoring, there is also less need for glucose monitoring test strips. However, the hybrid closed-loop system has also other costs: the insulin pump investment cost, infusion sets and their reservoirs, and continuous glucose monitoring sensors. On top of that, both methods also include several other costs that are similar with both: semiannual clinician control meetings and tests, glucose drops, snacks, freshen-up towels, blood glucose meters etc. The present daily basic treatment cost structures for both alternatives are presented in the following Table 1:

TABLE I.DAILY TREATMENT COST OF DIABETES WITH MDI AND CSII + CGM METHODS

	MDI	CSII + CGM
Insulin	1500	1200
Test strips	2000	1500
Other costs	1200	1200
Pump + transmitter		1400
Infusion sets & reservoirs		2400
Sensors		2160
Total annual costs (€)	4700	9860

The other part of the cost modeling was estimation of the long-term complication costs. These complications were categorized into 1) kidney problems (nephropathy), 2) vision problems (retinopathy), 3) work absence and early retirement costs, 4) nerve problems (neuropathy), 5) limb complications and 6) other complications. Of these six categories, the kidney problems, limb complications and work absence and early retirement costs are expected to be the most significant factors in future, given the expected development in early detection, avoidance, mitigation and advances in treatment of these

complications. Also, to varying degree, some of these complications, especially in the early stages, rather weaken the quality of life of the diabetic instead of causing significantly medical treatment costs.

The modeling was done so that the probability of the complications increases as a number of years go on. Then different annual costs were associated to each complication. These future costs are also subjective, as there is also significantly variance even today in estimating their true annual costs. For example, depending on the source, the annual costs of dialysis treatment of kidney failure are anywhere between €50 000 to €70 000. Also, the average cost for each amputation is over €70 000. The probabilities used in the analysis and results reported here are forward-looking and rather more optimistic than pessimistic, at least when compared with the current situation in Finland.

Modeling of the future complication treatment probabilities and costs is highly subjective. If diabetic people would pay more attention to their own well-being, they should also get significantly better treatment results with MDI/FIT than they do at the moment. There many adult T1D diabetics having HbA1c near or even below 6.5%, and those people are often also on the opinion that diabetes does not affect their life significantly, as they have learnt to have sufficiently healthy way of life, and FIT – flexible insulin therapy - treatment already gives them enough flexibility and freedom, as the name suggests. On the downside, there are people – diabetic and non-diabetic – who do not take good care of themselves. Drinking, smoking, overweight, lack of physical exercise, unhealthy diet, high blood pressure, bad cholesterol numbers, shift work, irregular way of life and many other things are not good either for healthy people. However, for diabetic people, unhealthy habits cause complications sooner than later. As the average results of HbA1c around 8.5% indicate [13], many patients do not take care of themselves well enough to avoid long-term complications.

The probability estimation for the complication costs in CSII + CGM hybrid closed-loop system is also difficult. In practice, if the diabetic uses the system correctly and has sufficiently healthy way of life, the diabetes treatment results should actually be so good that there are no complication costs. The devices will become even smarter over time, becoming more like artificial pancreases instead of being smart insulin pump systems. The results of the clinical tests are very promising, and some of the daring hackers have already reached safely such results that they were not even classified being diabetics based on their low HbA1c values (for more information on this, see e.g. www.dyips.org). Most of these results should be reached with products coming to the market already in 2017 or 2018 (e.g. Medtronic 670G), and this will only be the first cautionary step from one single manufacturer. The forthcoming models should definitely provide even better and easier treatment. Therefore, it is justified to assume that there are no long-term complication costs with hybrid closed-loop system (and with their successors, artificial pancreas systems). Actually, the systems should become so good that they will even surpass the results of some ordinary non-diabetic people.

VI. RESULTS

According to the simulation model results, the situation is quite obvious: under any foreseeable scenario or combination of parameters, the forth-coming CSII + CGM with hybrid closed-loop is always less expensive alternative for treatment according to the total lifetime costs, unless patient dies prematurely because of some non-diabetes related reason. It can be considered surprising that the difference between the two alternatives is so significant. For the MDI/FIT, the total discounted lifetime costs are ~ €900 000 while the costs with advanced CSII + CGM are ~ €320 000, approximately only one third in comparison with the MID treatment approach.

The following cumulative cost figure (Fig. 1) illustrates this situation best. Until having T1D approximately for 25 years, MDI/FIT approach is more cost-efficient alternative. This is because until that point, kidney complication and work absence costs have only emerged to those individuals who have not taken enough care of themselves. However, after that, more and more diabetics using MDI/FIT method require treatment for their complications. This naturally starts to increase the cumulative costs.

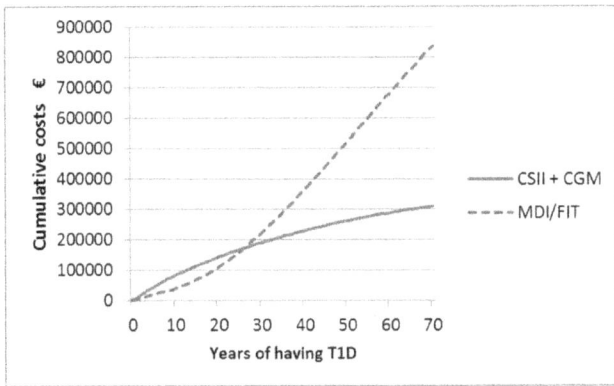

Fig. 1. Cumulative discounted total lifetime costs of MDI/FIT and advanced CSII+CGM method treatment. In the long run, CSII+CGM costs are lower because it practically eliminates the complication costs.

There is significantly variation around the expected value of CSII + CGM. This is can be explained with the fact that some people take good care of themselves, and thus do not suffer that much of the complication costs. On the other hand, these people also live longer, and thus their treatment costs also increase with time. This variation around the mean costs of MDI/FIT can be seen from the following Fig 2. For the CSII + CGM (not shown here with a graph), this deviation is of much smaller magnitude.

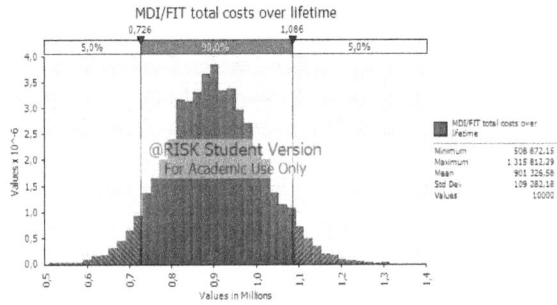

Fig. 2. Variation around the expected value of MDI/FIT method total costs over lifetime is significant because of the differing therapeutic control results achieved by type 1 diabetics.

One significant advantage of the forthcoming advanced CSII+CGM systems is that even if the diabetic does not bother to take treatment very seriously, the system will automatically re-balance the blood glucose level onto a specified level after some time delay. Therefore, even those people who are reluctant to take care of themselves are guaranteed to get sufficiently good treatment. This reduces complication risks, improves quality of life, and at the same time, saves tax payers' money.

Another significant advantage pointed out by some professionals was that there are many people who just cannot take care of themselves with MDI, and therefore they need assistance. Senior citizens with dementia and young children at kindergarten or at school are examples of such people. Use of CSII + CGM for diabetes treatment requires less special skills from the assistants. There are people who feel terrified if they need to assist some in injection of insulin. Doing the same dosing with CSII system is technically more like using of a smartphone, without need to see and use insulin pen needles.

The results and conclusions are quite obvious: new technology and diabetes treatment approach will be much more cost efficient in comparison with other currently existing methods. However, the presented numbers do not necessarily reflect the reality in the longer at all. There might become some completely new and revolutionary ways to medicate diabetes, and it is also possible that in the long run, scientists also find a way to cure diabetes.

VII. REAL OPTIONS IN THE CSII+CGM DEVELOPMENT

It turned out that even without real options, the novel CSII+CGM method is cost-wise a better alternative than MDI. Still, different real options, and also lack of them, were briefly analyzed from the qualitative perspective.

According to real option thinking, value of flexibility comes from uncertainty and value of waiting, and then making optimal decisions when there is more information available (Trigeorgis 1996). Most typical real option types are option to delay, option to switch, option to abandon, option to expand, growth options, option to contract investment size, option to switch between different alternatives, and staged investments [15].

There are three major reasons for the medical companies (both pharmaceutical drugs and device manufacturers) to enhance and fasten their R&D operations as much as possible: 1) market competition, 2) extinction of patents rights, and 3) use of external money in R&D activities. For example, in the USA only, insulin sales in 2011 totaled $8.3 billion, a 15% increase compared to 2010 (DDDI 2012) [16]. Therefore, every major medical company wants a share of this big and rapidly growing market. Patents for the synthetic human insulin expired in 2012, and also patent of the still commonly used long-term basal insulin analog, Lantus, expired in February 2015. If the existing companies are not active, newcomers might jeopardize the market with copied drugs. Therefore, there is no room to use option to delay.

There is a lot of money targeted to diabetes research and treatment. Therefore, it is rational to do R&D on nearly every considerable alternative, even on the more unlikely ways of treating diabetes, because funding for these projects comes partly from external sources, e.g. from different foundations. If something new turns out to be a hit, the upside potential is usually very high. As a result, every possible expansion and growth option is used whenever possible: it just part of the normal way of doing business. On the other hand, some R&D projects turn out to be failures: they are abandoned according to the common stage-gate models that are used commonly by major pharmaceutical companies (a policy partly dictated by the FDA as well).

The only area where the companies truly have different strengths is in the field of how to provide additional services to the users and other stakeholders. For example, manufacturers try to develop software to ease and encourage better self-management, and the physicians are given tools to analyze patient data. Also ability to monitor CGM in real time everywhere is high on the R&D list. Collecting physical exercise data is also essential to avoid hypoglycemia. A Finnish company Sensotrend, for example, is developing methods to estimate how much physical exercise affects the blood glucose balance, and how this information should be combined and used by the CSII + CGM hybrid closed-loop system. Manufacturers also develop software for smart phones and smart watches to make daily self-management easier than before.

As a result, there is a lot of real option type thinking and action in pharmaceutical companies. However, it has become part of their ordinary way of doing business. Also, unlike with traditional real options and financial options, uncertainty does not reveal itself without own active R&D. Secondly, competition means that there is no time to wait. It is essential to be in the market first. This is good news for diabetics as it guarantees that their treatment methods will continuously improve.

Another consideration in the beginning of the study was to consider if it would be feasible to wait until changing from the MDI/FIT treatment to the CSII + CGM, i.e., what is the optimal time of waiting until switching.

The answer for the value of delaying switching is zero, unless there is a new system coming in just a few months with better features (in which case it is obviously wise to wait).

However, the non-value of waiting to switch is related to how human mentality works. If diabetics get used to older methods and higher HbA1c target levels set for them, they are not mentally willing to improve their treatment quality even when it should be quite easy with improved methods. Another finding is that it is extremely important to take the treatment seriously from the very beginning. The first year impression affects strongly the willingness to take care of the disease for the rest of the life [17]. Therefore, physicians should encourage and guide the patients in the early stages of the disease. Giving precious treatment system with ambitious but achievable treatment target levels also signals diabetic the importance of following the medical treatment plan. New methods should also support better adherence and compliance, thus reducing the risk of diabetes self-management fatigue. Therefore, some physicians are on the opinion that in near future people with T1D, especially those not meeting their target levels, should use advanced CSII + CGM systems.

VIII. CONCLUSIONS

This paper compared the costs of treating diabetes type 1 with the currently used multiple daily injection (MDI/FIT) method and with the nascent method of combining insulin pump and continuous glucose monitoring (CSII + CGM) into a hybrid closed-loop system. The lifetime costs were modeled with simulated discounted cash flow method. Both direct and indirect costs of T1D treatment were considered.

The actual simulation model is quite straightforward, but getting reliable and accurate data as inputs is very difficult because depending on the source, there is variation even in the past data of cost estimations. Also, estimating the probabilities for different possible complications in future is difficult as there is still no precise knowledge on how different levels of HbA1c correlate with the complications in the long run over several decades.

The novel way of using CSII + CGM is in terms of costs is considerably less expensive alternative than MID/FIT (€900 000 vs. €320 000). This advantage stems from CSII + CGM systems' ability to semi-automatically adjust the blood glucose level to the optimal level even if the user is not strict on following the medical treatment plan. This eliminates nearly completely the long term complications and their costs. The daily basic treatment costs are about double in comparison with the MDI, but this is more than offset by the minimal indirect costs. Type 1 diabetics using MDI/FIT do not achieve on average sufficiently good therapeutic control, and therefore the indirect costs increase due to complications in kidneys, eyes, nerves, feet and cardiovascular system. Work absence and premature retirement also cause significant indirect costs.

For those with T1D, continuous development in the field of diabetes treatment is positive. Pharmaceutical industry and its real options were qualitatively analyzed to see if there are some reasons or obstacles that would give companies options to delay the development. However, expiring patents, hard market competition and external funding on R&D guarantees that every possible real option is used in a way that expedites the development. To set apart from their competitors, companies also need to improve and expand their products to have better offerings than their competitors. This will further enhance the development of advanced CSII + CGM hybrid closed-loop systems until we have an artificial pancreas - or cure for diabetes.

REFERENCES

[1] American Diabetes Association, "Economic Costs of Diabetes in the U.S. in 2012", Diabetes Care, March 2013, pp. 1 – 14.

[2] K. Reini, K. (2013), Diabetes Causes Substantial Losses for the Finnish Economy. National Institute for Health and Welfare, discussion paper, 14/2013.

[3] International Diabetes Federation's Diabetes Atlas (2011)

[4] T. Kangas, Diabeetikkojen terveyspalvelut ja niiden kustannukset. Helsinkiläisten diabeetikkojen verrokkikontrolloitu poikkileikkaustutkimus. Sosiaali- ja terveysturvan tutkimuksia 67. KELA; 2002.

[5] J. Lahtela, M. Saraheimo, I. Pasteranck, J. Isojärvi, A-K Himanen and S-L Hovi, (2012), "Insuliinipumppu aikuisten tyypin 1 diabeteksen hoidossa", Suomen Lääkärilehti 47/2012 vsk 67. pp. 3477-3484.

[6] www.diabetesliitto.fi

[7] P. Finne and C. Grönhagen-Riska, Suomen munuaistautirekisteri. Munuias- ja maksaliitto, 2013.

[8] M-T Saha, "Uusia upeita laitteita tulee omahoitoon – miksi potilaat eivät käytä niitä?", Diabetes ja lääkäri, huhtikuu 2015, pp. 16 – 17.

[9] D. Elleri, D. Dunger and R. Hovorka, "Closed-loop insulin delivery for treatment of type 1 diabetes", BMC Medicine 2011, 9:120.

[10] R. Miller, A. Secrest, R. Sharma and T. Songer, T. Orchard, "Improvements in the Life Expectancy of Type 1 Diabetes", Diabetes, Vol. 61, November 2012, pp. 2987 – 2992.

[11] S. Livingstone et al., "Estimated Life Expectancy in a Scottish Cohort With Type 1 Diabetes, 2008-2010", The Journal of the American Medical Association, January 6, 2015, Vol 313, No. 1.

[12] DCCT, "The Effect of Intensive Treatment of Diabetes on the Development and Progression of Long-Term Complications in Insulin-Dependent Diabetes Mellitus", The Diabetes Control and Complications Trial Research Group. New England Journal of Medicine, September 30, 1993, Vol. 329, pp. 977-986.

[13] T. Valle et al., Diabeetikkojen hoitotasapaino Suomessa vuosina 2009-2010. DEHKO-raportti 2010:5, Diabetesliitto.

[14] B. Tao, M. Pietropaolo, M. Atkinson, D. Schatz and D. Taylor, "Estimating the Cost of Type 1 Diabetes in the U.S.: A Propensity Score Matching Method." PLoS ONE 5(7): e11501. doi:10.1371/journal.pone.0011501.

[15] L. Trigeorgis, Real Options: Managerial Flexibility and Strategy in Resource Allocation. MIT Press, 1996.

[16] Diabetes drug and device industry 1Q12 financial model. San Francisco, Calif.,Close Concerns, Inc., 2012.

[17] T. Rönnemaa, "Tyypin 1 diabeetikoille ensimmäinen vuosi on erityisen tärkeä", Diabetes ja lääkäri, huhtikuu 2015, pp. 23 – 24.

Farm-Level Model of Short-Rotation Coppice Cultivation with Flexibility in Planting and Harvesting

Multi-stage Real Options Approach

Alisa Kostrova*, Robert Finger, Utkur Djanibekov

Institute for Food and Resource Economics, Chair of Production Economics

University of Bonn

Bonn, Germany

*Email: a.kostrova@ilr.uni-bonn.de

Abstract – Although short-rotation coppice (SRC) becomes of great significance worldwide due to increasing demand on energy and their significant advantages relative to competing agricultural crops, the estimated land capacity for SRC cultivation is hardly used in Germany. The results of models that have been developed to explain the observed reluctance of farmers to convert to SRC are controversial. Existing models are limited either to a hectare-based resolution, not taking into account farm's resource endowments and potential economies of scale, or to investments "now or never", not allowing to postpone any decision. We fill these gaps by developing a farm-level model for SRC cultivation and allowing for full flexibility in planting and harvesting, using the multi-stage real options approach. The model will be used to further understand the motivation of farmers and to evaluate different policy measures in order to stimulate conversion to SRC.

Keywords – perennial energy crops; farming decision; new investment theory.

I. INTRODUCTION

In the light of increasing demand on energy, bioenergy becomes of great significance worldwide [1, p.7], [2, p.16] with perennial energy crops having significant advantages over the conventional land use [3]. In particular, short rotation coppice (SRC)[1], as one type of perennial energy crops, is characterized by low-input production compering with competing crops [4]. In addition, there is a certain flexibility in SRC harvesting[2] that is possible at intervals of 2-20 years [5]. An optimum harvesting interval in terms of cost-benefit ratio exists due to the growth rate of SRC being a concave

function of the harvesting interval on the one hand, and increasing overtime harvesting costs on the other hand [6].

The potential area for SRC is large. For example, in Germany it is estimated as 5.7% (i.e. 680'000 hectares) of cropland and 33% (i.e. 1.5 Mio. hectares) of grassland, considering all restrictions [7], out of which only about 5'000 hectares are currently cultivated [8]. In order to stimulate the cultivation of SRC, an economic model is required that not only contributes to further understanding of farmers' motivation, but also allows evaluating the performance of different policy measures[3].

There have been a number of models developed to explain the observed reluctance of farmers to convert to SRC. However, they ignore either the farm-level constraints, operating on a hectare base, or flexibility in time of planting and harvesting. In this regard, the results of the previous studies are rather controversial, and there is no general agreement about profitability of SRC or efficiency of policy measures. In this paper we address the limitations of existing models. In particular, we develop a farm-level model of SRC cultivation and allow for full flexibility of planting and harvesting by using the multi-stage real options approach (ROA).

The outline is structured as follows. First, a brief overview of existing models with respect to SRC cultivation is given. Based on this, our research aim and hypotheses are formulated. Next, we introduce the concept of our model and provide a solution for it. We would like to emphasize that this

---

[1] Common plants suitable for SRC include poplar (*populus spp.*) and willow (*salix ssp.*) [4].

[2] Hereinafter we distinguish between an **intermediate harvesting**, i.e. the one, after which no replanting is needed, because the perennial energy crop continues to grow and can be harvested again in two years or later; and the **last harvesting**, i.e. complete clearance of the plantation. The rotation period, i.e. the time period between planting and the last harvesting, is restricted up to 20 years [5].

[3] Currently there is no additional support for SRC cultivation in Germany beyond the Greening of Common Agricultural Policy (CAP) of the European Union that reduces the direct payments to farmers by 30%, unless certain environmental requirements are fulfilled (those can be fulfilled among others by cultivation of SRC) [9]. However, the rural development policy allows the Member States to introduce some measures, supporting bioenergy production, e.g. adding value to biomass [10]. An example of currently implemented policy is the Energy Crops Scheme (ECS) in England [11].

is an outline of research in progress. Our next steps, as well as some issues to be discussed, are listed in the concluding part.

II. STATE OF THE ART

The results of economic evaluations of SRC found in the literature are quite heterogeneous. Out of 37 relevant studies 43% report economic viability of SRC; 19% - economic disadvantages; and 38% - mixed results [12]. The diversity of the results is explained not only by the different assumptions made, but also by the different theoretical frameworks applied [*ibid.*].

The theory that has been most frequently used to analyze the economy of SRC cultivation is the **classical investment theory**, e.g. [13]-[16]. The research is mainly devoted to the North American countries [17], [18] and to the Europe [19]–[21], including Germany [16], [22]. Since the approach doesn't allow postponing decision to convert, which might lead to an overestimation of conversion triggers [23, p.164], its relevance for analysis of SRC cultivation is rather questionable. This limitation has been tried to be overcome by using the new investment theory.

Despite the advantages of the **new investment theory** over the classical one and quite well developed theoretical background of the real options, the concept has been hardly applied to analyze the economic performance of perennial energy crops. Besides, the papers that use the ROA have limitations in several directions. They do not consider either flexibility in harvesting [24], or farm restrictions (i.e. analyzing the investment decision as stand-alone) [25], or both [23], [26], [27].

Other quantitative research have been conducted with respect to SRC cultivation, such as linear programming modelling [28], GIS-based spatial data analysis [29], [30], and supply-demand analysis [31], [32]. Among the **qualitative research** devoted to SRC cultivation are mainly farm surveys [33]–[35][4].

Thus, although a number of models have been developed to explain farmers' decision with respect to SRC cultivation, each of them is limited either to a hectare-based resolution, not taking into account potential farm's economy of scale, or to investments "now or never", not allowing to postpone any decision. Our paper aims to fill the gap by developing a farm-level model for SRC cultivation, and applying the multi-stage ROA[5] in order to allow for flexibility in both planting and harvesting.

There are three hypotheses of our research. First, based on previous research, demonstrating the profitability of SRC in terms of static NPV, and based on the observed reluctance to convert to SRC, we hypothesize that (1) under current conditions it is optimal to postpone the cultivation. Second,

based on the theoretical background of the ROA and [23], we hypothesize that, (2a) considering additionally flexibility of harvesting, we get a trigger value that is lower, than the one calculated allowing to postpone planting only, but (2b) higher than the one calculated according to the classical investment theory. Finally, we hypothesize that (3) taking into account farm-level constraints and possible economy of scale leads to a lower trigger value, comparing with the one derived from a hectare-based model.

III. MODEL AND SOLUTION

The first step is to generate cash flows, based on which the expanded NPV will be expressed and optimized subject to some farm-constraints[6]. The cash flows from cultivating SRC, denoted as $\pi(\cdot)$, are assumed to be stochastic and to follow a Geometric Brownian Motion (GBM) [36, pp.63–82].

The optimization problem can be described more generally as a problem of distributing a set of limited resources (in this section we assume there is only one limited resource, namely land L limited to $\bar{L}$) between two investment projects:

- Project A, or "Perennial Energy Crop" Project

   A multi-stage American option, where exercising the first stage (planting) requires the initial investment $I_A(L)$, and exercising every following stage (harvesting) earns immediate stochastic cash flow $\pi_t(L)$, which depends not only on the limited resources devoted to the project[7], but also on the time t. There must be at least two years between exercising two stages. Starting from the second stage (i.e. having exercised "planting") holding an option also binds a certain amount of the limited resources that might have been invested into the alternative project. In other words, holding an option incurs some opportunity costs annually. In addition, at every stage, starting from the second one, the investment project can be stopped for some additional costs θ (the last harvesting), and the limited resources can be taken out of the project.

- Project B, or "Traditional Agriculture" Project

   A one-year risk-free investment project that requires initial investments resulting in revenue in the following period. Both – the initial investments and the revenue – depend on the limited resources, distributed to the project. The project can be re-exercised every year.

The net present value of the Project B, denoted as $NPV_B(L)$, is derived under the assumption of optimum use of

---

[4] Although we don't use these methods as a basis for our model, we do take the results obtained in these papers into consideration, for instance in setting up the assumptions of our model.

[5] We assume that the first "Harvesting" is an option on an option "Planting", and each following "Harvesting" is an option on the previous one; that is basically the multi-stage real options.

[6] The farm constraints might include availability of land area of each soil type, labor and machinery capacity, liquidity and etc.

[7] We assume a non-linear function of stochastic cash flow with respect to the limited resource. Otherwise the result of the maximization problem would be a corner solution, i.e. to devote the whole limited resource either to the Project A or to the Project B.

resources for traditional agriculture and is a function (linear or non-linear) of the limited resources. Since we assume there is no risk and flexibility related to the Project B, its net present value is calculated according to the classical investment theory.

The option values of all stages of the Project A, denoted as $V_n(\pi(L))$ with $n \in \{1,2,...,N\}$ and N being the total number of stages, are calculated using the multi-stage ROA. The trigger cash flows for exercising each stage are denoted as $\pi_n^*(L)$ and have to satisfy $\pi_n^*(L) \leq \pi_{n-1}^*(L)$ for all n. We present here the solution for the case $N = 2$. The other cases can be solved in a similar way[8].

In the case $N = 2$ there are two stages only: planting and the last harvesting. The two value functions have to satisfy the differential equations (respectively):

$$\frac{1}{2}\sigma^2\pi^2(L)V_1''(\pi(L)) + (r - \delta)\pi(L)V_1'(\pi(L)) \\ -rV_1(\pi(L)) = 0 \tag{1}$$

$$\frac{1}{2}\sigma^2\pi^2(L)V_2''(\pi(L)) + (r - \delta)\pi(L)V_2'(\pi(L)) \\ -rV_2(\pi(L)) - NPV_B(L) = 0 \tag{2}$$

where

σ – variance of the GBM (cash flows of SRC);
$V'(\cdot)$ and $V''(\cdot)$ are the first and the second derivatives respectively;
r - risk-free discount rate (continuous);
μ - risk-adjusted discount rate (continuous);
α – drift rate of the GBM (cash flows of SRC);
$\delta = \mu - \alpha$.

The value functions should have the forms:

$$V_1(\pi(L)) = A_1\pi^{\beta_1}(L) \tag{3}$$

$$V_2(\pi(L)) = B_1\pi^{\beta_1}(L) + B_2\pi^{\beta_2}(L) - \frac{NPV_B(L)}{r} \tag{4}$$

where
A_1, B_1 and B_2 are non-negative constants to be defined;

$\beta_1 = \frac{1}{2} - \frac{\mu-\delta}{\sigma^2} + \sqrt{[\frac{\mu-\delta}{\sigma^2} - \frac{1}{2}]^2 + \frac{2\mu}{\sigma^2}} > 1$;

$\beta_2 = \frac{1}{2} - \frac{\mu-\delta}{\sigma^2} - \sqrt{[\frac{\mu-\delta}{\sigma^2} - \frac{1}{2}]^2 + \frac{2\mu}{\sigma^2}} < 0$;

$-\frac{NPV_B(L)}{r}$ is a particular solution of the nonhomogeneous differential equation (2).

The value-matching conditions are

$$V_1(\pi_1^*(L)) = V_2(2\alpha\pi_1^*(L)) * e^{-2r} \\ -I_A(L) - NPV_B(L) * e^{-r} \tag{5}$$

$$V_2(\pi_2^*(L)) = \pi_2^*(L) - \theta(L) \tag{6}$$

where
e – the Euler number.

Equation (5) means that in two years after exercising the first stage (planting) the investor gets the second one (the last harvesting), however, losing the opportunity costs of the alternative project inbetween. In addition, in order to exercise the first stage the initial investments have to be made. Equation (6) means that after exercising the second stage, the investor immediately obtains the profit from harvesting, covering additional costs for quitting the project.

The smooth-pasting conditions are

$$V_1'(\pi_1^*(L)) = V_2'(2\alpha\pi_1^*(L)) * e^{-2r} \tag{7}$$

$$V_2'(\pi_2^*(L)) = 1 \tag{8}$$

Having derived the net present values of both projects independently as functions of the limited resources, the investor maximizes his/her **total net present value** by distributing the limited resources between the two projects and by choosing the timing for the first one. The output of this maximization is the shares of limited resources distributed to each project. We distinguish between the time periods of exercising the stages of the Project A[9]:

- Time $t \in \{0, 1, ..., t_1\}$ with t_1 being the time period of exercising the first stage of the Project A

$$NPV_{[0;t_1]}(L_A) = \left[\sum_{s=0}^{t_1} V_1(\pi_s(\bar{L}), \bar{L}) * e^{-rs}\right] \\ -I_A(L_A) * e^{-rt_1} - NPV_B(L_A) * e^{-r(t_1+1)} \tag{9}$$

where
$NPV_B(L_A)$ – the opportunity costs of the Project B.

As long as the cash flow of the Project A is below the trigger value $\pi_1^*(L_A)$, all the limited resources are invested into the Project B and the option to exercise the first stage of the Project A is held. Note that the opportunity costs of the Project B are already considered in the option values of the Project A. Once the cash flow of the Project A exceeds the trigger value (assume this happens in the time period t_1), the first stage of the Project A is exercised, requiring the initial investment immediately and the opportunity costs of the alternative project in the following period, and obtaining the option to exercise the second stage of the Project A in two years.

- Time $t \in \{t_{n-1} + 2, ..., t_n\}$ with t_n being the time period of exercising the nth stage of the Project A

$$NPV_{[t_{n-1}+2;t_n]}(L_A) = \left[\sum_{s=t_{n-1}+2}^{t_n} V_n(\pi_s(L_A), L_A) * e^{-rs}\right] \\ +\pi_{t_n}(L_A) * e^{-rt_n} - NPV_B(L_A) * e^{-r(t_n+1)} \tag{10}$$

---

[8] The provided way of solving is based on [36].

[9] Hereinafter we are back to the general case, when the number of stages is N.

Holding every option between the first and the last one (i.e. an option of intermediate harvesting), the investor gets the net present value of this option. Once he/she exercises an intermediate stage (at time t_n), he/she gets a cash flow immediately, but has to incur the opportunity costs of the alternative project in the following period.

- Time $t \in \{t_{N-1} + 2, ..., t_N\}$ with t_N being the time period of exercising the last stage (i.e. the Nth stage) of the Project A

$$NPV_{[t_{N-1}+2;t_N]}(L_A) = \left[\sum_{s=t_{N-1}+2}^{t_N} V_N(\pi_s(L_A), L_A) * e^{-rs} \right] \quad (11)$$
$$+ \left[\pi_{t_N}(L_A) - \theta(L_A) \right] * e^{-rt_N}$$

Exercising the last option in the time period t_N, and therefore taking the limited resource out of the Project A, the investor gets a cash flow and pays some costs for quitting immediately, and has no more any opportunity costs of the alternative project in the following period.

So, the total NPV over the time period $[0; t_N]$ is

$$NPV = NPV_{[0;t_1]}(L_A)$$
$$+ \left[\sum_{n=2}^{N-1} NPV_{[t_{n-1}+2;t_n]}(L_A) * e^{-rt_n} \right] \quad (12)$$
$$+ NPV_{[t_{N-1}+2;t_N]}(L_A) * e^{-r(t_{N-1}+2)}$$
$$\xrightarrow[0 \leq L_A \leq \bar{L}, \ t_0, \ \{t_n\}, \ t_N \leq 20]{} max!$$

which is maximized over the limited resources devoted to the Project A and over the timing of the Project A.

The primary source of data used to derive farm-level information required for the above model is [5]. The missing data are taken from the existing literature. After developing and testing the model, we will check our hypotheses and evaluate the effects of different policy measures on SRC cultivation.

IV. CONCLUSION

Short-rotation coppice becomes of great significance worldwide due to increasing demand on energy and due to significant advantages over other bioenergy crops. However, in Germany the estimated potential area of land for SRC cultivation is far beyond the currently used one.

There have been a number of models developed to explain the observed reluctance of farmers to convert to SRC, being however limited and producing controversial output. To our knowledge, there has been no farm-level model developed for perennial energy crops that considers flexibility in both planting and harvesting.

We developed a farm-level model for SRC cultivation that allows for full flexibility in planting and harvesting, using the multi-stage ROA. In particular, we provided a solution for a problem of distributing a set of limited resources between two investment projects: a multi-stage American option (i.e. cultivation of perennial energy crops) and a one-period risk-free investment project (i.e. traditional agriculture). The model will be used to further understand the motivation of farmers and to evaluate different policy measures in order to stimulate conversion to SRC.

In our next research steps we focus on finalizing the solution of the model and providing a numerical example. However, there are still open questions, the main one out of which is how to derive the number of stages N and timing for the "Perennial Energy Crop" Project from the model. An option could be to run the model for different number of stages N and then choose the optimal one, i.e. to provide not a closed-form solution, but an analytical one.

REFERENCES

[1] J. Zeddies, E. Bahrs, N. Schoenleber, and W. Gamer, "Globale Analyse und Abschätzung des Biomasse-Flächennutzungspotentials," Aug-2012. [Online]. Available: https://www.uni-hohenheim.de/i410b/download/publikationen/Globale%20Biomassepotenziale%20_%20FNR%2022003911%20Zwischenbericht%202012.pdf. [Accessed: 09-Feb-2015].

[2] J. Muehlenhof, "Anbau von Energiepflanzen. Umweltauswirkungen, Nutzungskonkurrenzen und Potenziale.," Apr-2013. [Online]. Available: http://www.unendlich-viel-energie.de/media/file/166.65_Renews_Spezial_Energiepflanzen_apr13.pdf. [Accessed: 09-Feb-2015].

[3] A. Monti, S. Fazio, and G. Venturi, "Cradle-to-farm gate life cycle assessment in perennial energy crops," Eur. J. Agron., vol. 31, no. 2, pp. 77–84, Aug-2009.

[4] R. J. Faasch and G. Patenaude, "The economics of short rotation coppice in Germany," Biomass Bioenergy, vol. 45, pp. 27–40, Oct-2012.

[5] Kuratorium für Technik und Bauwesen in der Landwirtschaft e.V., Energiepflanzen : Daten für die Planung des Energiepflanzenanbaus, 2nd ed. Darmstadt, Germany: KTBL, 2012.

[6] G. Deckmyn, I. Laureysens, J. Garcia, B. Muys, and R. Ceulemans, "Poplar growth and yield in short rotation coppice: model simulations using the process model SECRETS," Biomass Bioenergy, vol. 26, no. 3, pp. 221–227, Mar-2004.

[7] C. Aust, J. Schweier, F. Brodbeck, U. H. Sauter, G. Becker, and J.-P. Schnitzler, "Land availability and potential biomass production with poplar and willow short rotation coppices in Germany," GCB Bioenergy, vol. 6, no. 5, pp. 521–533, Sep-2014.

[8] A. Bemmann and C. Knust, Kurzumbetriebsplantagen in Deutschland und europäische Perspektiven. Berlin, Germany: Weißensee Verlag, 2010.

[9] Bundesministerium fuer Ernaehrung und Landwirtschaft, "EU-Agrarpolitik - FAQ zur Agrarreform und der nationalen Umsetzung," 24-Feb-2015. [Online]. Available: http://www.bmel.de/DE/Landwirtschaft/Agrarpolitik/_Texte/GAP-FAQs.html;jsessionid=0D73EAAFA1620445FB82F36E765C5694.2_cid296#doc4121226bodyText8. [Accessed: 29-May-2015].

[10] European Commission, Council Regulation (EC) No 73/2009 of 19 January 2009 establishing common rules for direct support schemes for farmers under the common agricultural policy and establishing certain support schemes for farmers, amending Regulations (EC) No 1290/2005, (EC) No 247/2006, (EC) No 378/2007 and repealing Regulation (EC) No 1782/2003. 2009. [Online]. Available: http://eur-lex.europa.eu/legal-content/en/TXT/?uri=CELEX:32009R0073. [Accessed: 22-May-2015].

[11] Natural England, "Energy Crops Scheme: terms and conditions of your agreement - Detailed guidance," 09-Nov-2014. [Online]. Available: https://www.gov.uk/energy-crops-scheme-terms-and-conditions-of-your-agreement. [Accessed: 22-May-2015].

[12] S. Hauk, T. Knoke, and S. Wittkopf, "Economic evaluation of short rotation coppice systems for energy from biomass—A review," *Renew. Sustain. Energy Rev.*, vol. 29, pp. 435–448, Jan-2014.

[13] D. C. Lothner, H. M. Hoganson, and P. A. Rubin, "Examining short-rotation hybrid poplar investments by using stochastic simulation," *Can. J. For. Res.*, vol. 16, no. 6, pp. 1207–1213, Dec-1986.

[14] C. H. Strauss, S. C. Grado, P. R. Blankenhorn, and T. W. Bowersox, "Economic evaluations of multiple rotation sric biomass plantations," *Sol. Energy*, vol. 41, no. 2, pp. 207–214, 1988.

[15] M. Gandorfer, K. Eckstein, and H. Hoffmann, "Modeling Economic Performance of an Agroforestry System under Yield and Price Risk.," presented at the Paper prepared for presentation at the 15th International Consortium on Applied Bioeconomy Research (ICABR) Annual Conference1, 2011. [Online]. Available: http://mediatum.ub.tum.de/node?id=1197218. [Accessed: 16-Apr-2015].

[16] J. Schweier and G. Becker, "Economics of poplar short rotation coppice plantations on marginal land in Germany," *Biomass Bioenergy*, vol. 59, pp. 494–502, Dec-2013.

[17] D. C. Lothner, "Short-Rotation Energy Plantations in North Central United States: An Economic Analysis," *Energy Sources*, vol. 13, no. 1, pp. 111–117, Jan-1991.

[18] D. W. McKenney, D. Yemshanov, S. Fraleigh, D. Allen, and F. Preto, "An economic assessment of the use of short-rotation coppice woody biomass to heat greenhouses in southern Canada," *Biomass Bioenergy*, vol. 35, no. 1, pp. 374–384, Jan-2011.

[19] J.-E. Bergez, L. Bouvarel, and D. Auclair, "Short rotation forestry: An agricultural case study of economic feasibility," *Bioresour. Technol.*, vol. 35, no. 1, pp. 41–47, 1991.

[20] K. Ericsson, H. Rosenqvist, E. Ganko, M. Pisarek, and L. Nilsson, "An agro-economic analysis of willow cultivation in Poland," *Biomass Bioenergy*, vol. 30, no. 1, pp. 16–27, Jan-2006.

[21] C. M. Gasol, F. Brun, A. Mosso, J. Rieradevall, and X. Gabarrell, "Economic assessment and comparison of acacia energy crop with annual traditional crops in Southern Europe," *Energy Policy*, vol. 38, no. 1, pp. 592–597, Jan-2010.

[22] M. Kroeber, K. Hank, J. Heinrich, and P. Wagner, "Ermittlung der Wirtschaftlichkeit der Energieholzanbaua in Kurzumbetriebslantagen - Risikoanalyse mit Hilfe der Monte-Carlo-Simulation," presented at the GEWISOLA „Risiken in der Agrar- und Ernährungswirtschaft und ihre Bewältigung", Bonn, Germany, 24-Sep-2008. [Online]. Available: http://core.ac.uk/download/pdf/6570052.pdf. [Accessed: 16-Apr-2015].

[23] M. Wolbert-Haverkamp and O. Musshoff, "Are short rotation coppices an economically interesting form of land use? A real options analysis," *Land Use Policy*, vol. 38, pp. 163–174, May-2014.

[24] F. Bartolini and D. Viaggi, "An analysis of policy scenario effects on the adoption of energy production on the farm: A case study in Emilia–Romagna (Italy)," *Energy Policy*, vol. 51, pp. 454–464, Dec-2012.

[25] G. E. Frey, D. E. Mercer, F. W. Cubbage, and R. C. Abt, "A real options model to assess the role of flexibility in forestry and agroforestry adoption and disadoption in the Lower Mississippi Alluvial Valley," *Agric. Econ.*, vol. 44, no. 1, pp. 73–91, Jan-2013.

[26] O. Musshoff, "Growing short rotation coppice on agricultural land in Germany: A Real Options Approach," *Biomass Bioenergy*, vol. 41, pp. 73–85, Jun-2012.

[27] F. Song, J. Zhao, and S. M. Swinton, "Switching to Perennial Energy Crops Under Uncertainty and Costly Reversibility," *Am. J. Agric. Econ.*, vol. 93, no. 3, pp. 768–783, Apr-2011.

[28] C. Sherrington and D. Moran, "Modelling farmer uptake of perennial energy crops in the UK," *Energy Policy*, vol. 38, no. 7, pp. 3567–3578, Jul-2010.

[29] A. Thomas, A. Bond, and K. Hiscock, "A GIS based assessment of bioenergy potential in England within existing energy systems," *Biomass Bioenergy*, vol. 55, pp. 107–121, Aug-2013.

[30] M. Stork, A. Schulte, and D. Murach, "Large-scale fuelwood production on agricultural fields in mesoscale river catchments – GIS-based determination of potentials in the Dahme river catchment (Brandenburg, NE Germany)," *Biomass Bioenergy*, vol. 64, pp. 42–49, May-2014.

[31] P. Alexander, D. Moran, M. D. A. Rounsevell, and P. Smith, "Modelling the perennial energy crop market: the role of spatial diffusion," *J. R. Soc. Interface*, vol. 10, no. 88, p. 20130656, Nov-2013.

[32] P. Alexander, D. Moran, P. Smith, A. Hastings, S. Wang, G. Sünnenberg, A. Lovett, M. J. Tallis, E. Casella, G. Taylor, J. Finch, and I. Cisowska, "Estimating UK perennial energy crop supply using farm-scale models with spatially disaggregated data," *GCB Bioenergy*, vol. 6, no. 2, pp. 142–155, Mar-2014.

[33] D. J. Smith, C. Schulman, D. Current, and K. W. Easter, "Willingness of Agricultural Landowners to Supply Perennial Energy Crops," in *Selected Paper*, Pittsburgh, Pennsylvania, 2011, p. 31.

[34] N. J. Glithero, P. Wilson, and S. J. Ramsden, "Prospects for arable farm uptake of Short Rotation Coppice willow and miscanthus in England," *Appl. Energy*, vol. 107, no. 100, pp. 209–218, Jul-2013.

[35] S. Hauk, S. Wittkopf, and T. Knoke, "Analysis of commercial short rotation coppices in Bavaria, southern Germany," *Biomass Bioenergy*, vol. 67, pp. 401–412, Aug-2014.

[36] A. K. Dixit and R. S. Pindyck, Investment Under Uncertainty. Princeton University Press, 1994.

Comparing Datar-Mathews and fuzzy pay-off approaches to real option valuation

Mariia Kozlova, Mikael Collan, and Pasi Luukka

School of Business and Management

Lappeenranta University of Technology

Lappeenranta, Finland

Mariia.Kozlova@lut.fi

Abstract—The paper is designed to compare two real option valuation techniques, Datar-Mathews method based on the probabilistic approach and a fuzzy pay-off method based on the possibilistic theory. These approaches comprise similar logic, recognizing the whole investment project as a real option, if investment can be terminated in case of loss forecast. Real option value is defined as a risk adjusted expected mean of the positive side of the resulting outcome distribution. Simple intuition makes these methods attractive for investment analysis. However, being relatively young they have not spread deeply to business practice and academic research. Possessing identic logic but utilizing different theoretical foundations these techniques are especially interesting to compare.

In general, results obtained from applying these methods to real option analysis are consistent. Simple triangular possibilistic distribution appears to overly simplify an investment case with complex interaction of uncertain factors. However, possibilistic theory provides grounds for further method extension. Fuzzy inference rules applied to outcomes resulting from different combinations of uncertain factors create an aggregate possibilistic distribution that joins features of real option and sensitivity analyses. This enables to trace interconnections of uncertain factors to particular ranges of investment pay-off, facilitating and deepening investment analysis.

Keywords—real option valuation; Datar-Mathews method; fuzzy pay-off method; fuzzy inference.

I. INTRODUCTION

Real option analysis is slowly becoming a part of investment planning in companies [1, 2] and it has been gaining more and more attention in academia. Different types of real options (RO) are recognized and different approaches exist to value them [3]. The problem of RO valuation was initially addressed with the models originally designed for the valuation of financial options, Black-Scholes formula [4] and binomial option pricing techniques [5]. Today business users of real option valuation are moving away from using these "original" models and (Monte Carlo) simulation based real option valuation [6-8], fuzzy real option valuation methods [9-12], and system dynamic modeling as a basis of real option valuation [13] are gaining ground in the industry. The different RO analysis methods are not competitors to each other, as the selection of the model used should be made based on the type

of uncertainty surrounding the analyzed investment and based on the available information [14].

However, two novel real option valuation methods possess identical valuation logic, but different theoretical background. Datar-Mathews method (DMM) exploits Monte-Carlo simulation representing investment profitability with probability distribution [6-8]. Whereas fuzzy pay-off method (FPOM) addresses uncertainty with possibilistic distribution or a fuzzy number [9-12]. Being emerging approaches they have not spread widely to the academia and business yet.

This paper focuses on the two mentioned methods, DMM and FPOM, aiming to apply them on a virtual investment case and compare the results. The investment case is chosen in a way to provide complex interaction of influential factors. It is represented by solar photovoltaic (PV) power plant investment project, benefiting not only from electricity sales but also from capacity payments. The latter is a function of a number of factors including variable market conditions and particular project peculiarities, creating a complicated network of causal relationships.

The investment model is built to analyze profitability of the solar PV project. The same investment model provides a basis for both Monte Carlo simulation for implementing DMM and scenario calculation for FPOM. The results of each valuation technique including characteristics of distribution and descriptive statistics are examined and compared. Inability of both methods to trace what combinations of uncertain factors end up in different ranges of project pay-off is revealed. In order to cover this gap, possible extensions of each method analysis were investigated. As the result, fuzzy inference rules are adapted to FPOM leading to a complex possibilistic distribution that is able to illustrate relationship between different uncertainty sources and the project outcome.

Such kind of comparison of these real option valuation methods is for the first time presented to the academic and business community. Elaborated fuzzy pay-off method extension with fuzzy inference rules represents a next step in real option valuation and more generally investment analysis.

This paper continues with section II introducing brief literature review and the general theory behind analyzing methods. The next part, Results, demonstrates and compares the main outputs of the application of the two methods and provides insights on their extension. Finally, Conclusion discusses findings, their implications, limitations, and suggestions for future research.

II. BACKGROUND

In this part, we briefly describe the theoretical foundations of the real option valuation methods, DMM and FPOM, enlightening their computational logic.

A. Datar-Mathews method

Intention to handle series of investment projects uniformly fostered a new intuitive approach of real option valuation named after its authors the Datar-Mathews method (DMM) [6]. The whole investment project is referred as a real option, if investment can be terminated in case of loss forecast.

Project profitability variation is analyzed by means of the Monte Carlo simulation with randomized input variables. Resulting probability distribution is a key element for further real option valuation. Since all negative outcomes of the project can be terminated, in the next step so called project Payoff Distribution is created. It is obtained by deducting the launch cost from the operating profit distribution, mapping all negative outcomes as zero, and weighting positive outcomes on the success ratio (the ratio of the successful outcomes to all probable outcomes). The mean of the resulting pay-off distribution is a real option value. Authors define it as 'Risk Adjusted Success Probability x (Benefits – Costs)' [6].

This algorithm reflects the general intuition behind the real option concept that RO is the right, but not the obligation. DMM is proved especially viable for investment cases with severe initial risk profile but potentially high returns in the long run. The Datar-Mathews method was successfully utilized by the Boeing Corporation, enhancing its ability of contingency planning and strategic thinking [6].

B. Fuzzy pay-off method

The same valuation logic is incorporated to the fuzzy pay-off method (FPOM), however, instead of probability distribution, authors adapt possibility distribution or a fuzzy number as representation of project profitability. Such replacement substantially facilitates the computational procedure. FPOM requires calculating only three scenarios (in a simple case) as opposed to thousands of iterations needed for the Monte Carlo simulation. The fuzzy number arises from assigning zero possibility to extreme (pessimistic and optimistic) scenarios and full possibility equal to one to the middle realistic scenario. The former two form the borders of all possible outcomes and are assigned with zero membership degree. As the result, triangular possibility distribution evolves (Fig. 1).

Real option value is defined as the fuzzy mean of the positive area of this distribution $E(A_+)$ weighted on the success ratio (the ratio of the positive area A_+ to the whole area A of the distribution) (1).

$$ROV = E(A^+) * \frac{A^+}{A} \qquad (1)$$

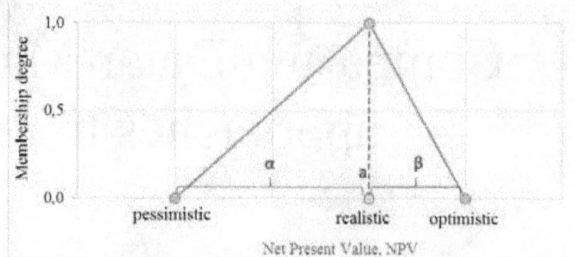

Fig. 1. Classical triangular fuzzy pay-off distribution.

The definition and derivation of the fuzzy mean is given in [15]. Practically, the fuzzy mean of the positive side of the distribution and the success ratio are calculated differently depending on the position of the distribution with relation to zero.

- When the whole distribution is in the positive zone, success ratio is equal to 1 and fuzzy mean of the positive area is the same as fuzzy mean of the whole distribution ($E(A)$):

$$E(A) = E(A^+) = a + \frac{\beta - \alpha}{6}, \qquad (2)$$

where a is a realistic net present value (NPV),

α is a distance between realistic and pessimistic NPV, and

β is a distance between realistic and optimistic NPV as presented in Fig. 1.

- If zero lies between realistic and optimistic NPV:

$$E(A^+) = \frac{(\alpha + \beta)^3}{6\beta^2} \qquad (3)$$

- If zero lies between pessimistic and realistic NPV:

$$E(A^+) = a + \frac{\beta - \alpha}{6} + \frac{(\alpha - a)^3}{6\alpha^2} \qquad (4)$$

- Finally, if the whole distribution is in the negative zone, $E(A^+)$ is equal to zero.

The success ratio is defined in all these cases based on the ordinary geometric rules.

Both approaches, DMM and FPOM, encompass the same logic treating the whole investment project as a real option, but different implementation foundations, the probability theory in case of DMM and the possibility theory (or the fuzzy set theory) in case of FPOM.

Being amongst the latest developments on the real option valuation, DMM and FPOM appear not to have spread widely in the academic literature yet. The Datar-Mathews method is demonstrated mostly in relation to some Boeing's investment cases [6, 7, 16]. The fuzzy pay-off method application is limited to several real-word problems in corporate finance, including pre-acquisition screening of target companies [17], patent valuation [11, 18], and R&D selection [19]. These methods have not been applied simultaneously to the same investment cases, except merely in [20]. With an exception of apparent difference in computational procedure, DMM and FPOM attributes have not been compared thoroughly. Different nature of their theoretical foundation can potentially lead to diverse capabilities and contribution to investment analysis that creates a need for a comparative study.

III. RESULTS

A. Numerical case illustration

The investment model is built for an industrial-scale solar PV power plant, which revenues comprise of electricity sales in the Russian wholesale energy market and capacity payments. The latter is calculated by the regulating authority as a variable rate annuity designed to provide a certain level of return on investment, taking into account altering market conditions and project-specific characteristics [21, 22]. Capacity revenue partly offsets dependence form electricity prices, inflation and interest rate, while posing a limit on capital expenditures (CapEx), setting target electricity production performance (target capacity factor), and imposing localization requirement (requirement to obtain equipment and services produced locally in Russia). Detailed description of the case and assumptions can be found in [20].

Project profitability is represented by its NPV obtained from the classical cash flow calculation performed by means of Microsoft Excel®. The fuzzy pay-off method is implemented based on this model with assumptions for three scenarios as shown in the Table 1. Real option valuation is performed in accordance with foundations provided in the section II. Monte Carlo simulation for the Data-Mathews method is realized with Matlab Simulink®, where identical cash flow model is built. Uncertain variables are assumed random numbers uniformly distributed between the extreme values specified in the Table 1 (values for the pessimistic and optimistic scenarios). The model runs simulation 10000 times and displays resulting NPVs as a probability distribution. Omitting the DMM step of creating the Payoff Distribution, the model goes straight to the real option valuation as a probability weighted mean of the positive area of the distribution multiplied by the success ratio that is consistent with DMM valuation logic.

B. Comparative analysis of the methods

Fig. 2 introduces the results obtained with the Datar-Mathews method (a), with the fuzzy pay-off method (b), and their convergence (c). The latter clearly demonstrates distribution borders matching. However, the shape of the probability distribution is intricately dissected that is attributed to the complex interaction of uncertain factors.

Whereas ordinary triangular form of the possibility distribution seems to overly simplify the case.

First two graphs of Fig. 2 display the real option value (with green) and probability-weighted and fuzzy mean (with red). These and some other descriptive statistics are also presented in the Table 2. The results show the difference between valuation techniques, as FPOM states substantially lower RO value, mean NPV (in absolute values) and standard deviation, and higher success ration as opposed to DMM. Such difference is partly caused by diversity of the theoretical foundations of the two methods, and partly by the simpler form of the possibility distribution that dislocates weights closer to the realistic scenario comparing to the probability distribution that has several peaks.

C. Extensions of the methods

The probability distribution in Fig. 2 might seem to comprise more information about the investment than the possibility distribution. The right peak that encompasses positive NPVs represents desirable outcomes, while the rest of the distribution signifies large risks associated with the project. Apparent disadvantage of such distribution is inability to show what combination of factors results in positive net present values. The only way to examine it is to play with the model, changing random inputs one by one. However, such procedure is time consuming and does not guarantee full understanding of the case. Contrary, the possibilistic approach possesses some potential in this sense.

Triangular shape of the possibility distribution makes perfect sense when uncertain factors affect the outcome uniformly along their possible range, as electricity price and inflation in the current case. Specific effects of the electricity production performance on the capacity payments and consequently on the project profitability suggest necessity of different treatment. This influence splits precisely to the three different levels – full capacity payments if capacity factor reaches more than 75% of the legislative target, 80% capacity payments if capacity factor falls between 50 and 75% of the target, and no capacity payments otherwise. These levels can actually represent distinct cases of power plant siting characterized by different solar irradiation. Hence, we can represent them with three possibility distributions instead of one.

Detailing of the resulting picture can be deepened further. Within each of the three triangular distributions there is still some combinations of factors that would beneficial to reveal.

TABLE 1. UNCERTAIN FACTORS

Factor	Range of values		
	Pessimistic	*Realistic*	*Optimistic*
Electricity price, rub./MWh	1000	2000	3000
Consumer price index (inflation)	1.70	1.35	1.00
CapEx level	150%	100%	80%
Capacity factor (percent of target)	30%	75%	120%
Localization requirement	Failed	Fulfilled	Fulfilled

TABLE 2. COMPARISON OF RESULTING STATISTICS (THOUS.RUB.)

Factor	Descriptive statistics		Difference
	DMM	*FPOM*	
Real option value	4192	2037	-51%
Mean NPV	-524862	-261359	-50%
Standard deviation	441292	357602	-19%
Success ratio	3%	9%	200%

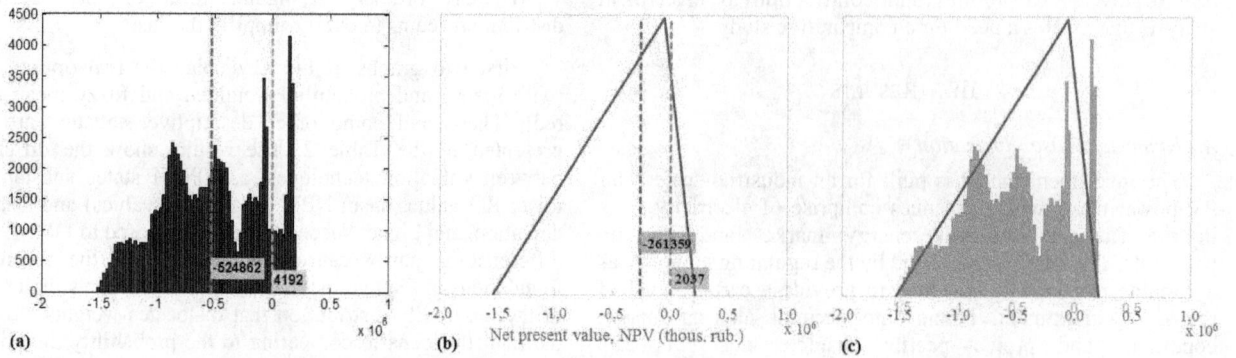

Fig. 2. Net present value distribution. (a) Probability, (b) possibility distribution, and (c) their convergence.
(red – mean NPV, green – real option value.)

It is fulfilling localization requirement that has only to discrete values and capital costs, which increase is partly offset by rising of capacity payments, but only until the limit. Thus, we should consider two different situations with respect to localization and two another different situations with respects to CapEx, resulting in four possible combinations of these factors.

Each of the four combinations can be represented by stand-alone triangular distribution. In order to differentiate between them, we apply fuzzy inference rules, assumptions for which are shown in the Table 3. Triangles that represent different combinations would be simply cut at different height in accordance with these rules. Resulting figures can be further combined by taking fuzzy union of their membership degree functions as defined in (2) for fuzzy sets A and B.

$$\mu_{A \cup B} = max\{\mu_A; \mu_B\}, \qquad (2)$$

Fig. 3 illustrates gradually these operations. Firstly, we present a case with capacity factor higher than 75% of the target as a separate possibilistic distribution (Fig. 3 (a)). All other factors stay fuzzy as defined previously in Table 1. Secondly, this distribution is divided into four separate distributions, each representing different combinations of fulfilling CapEx limit and localization requirement (Fig. 3 (b)). The left distribution illustrates the case when both requirements are failed as specified on the bottom of the graph, the right one shows the opposite situation and two distributions in the middle represent two combinations of these conditions when one is reached and another is failed. Other factors have the same values across all four distributions in corresponding scenarios (pessimistic, realistic, and optimistic). In particular,

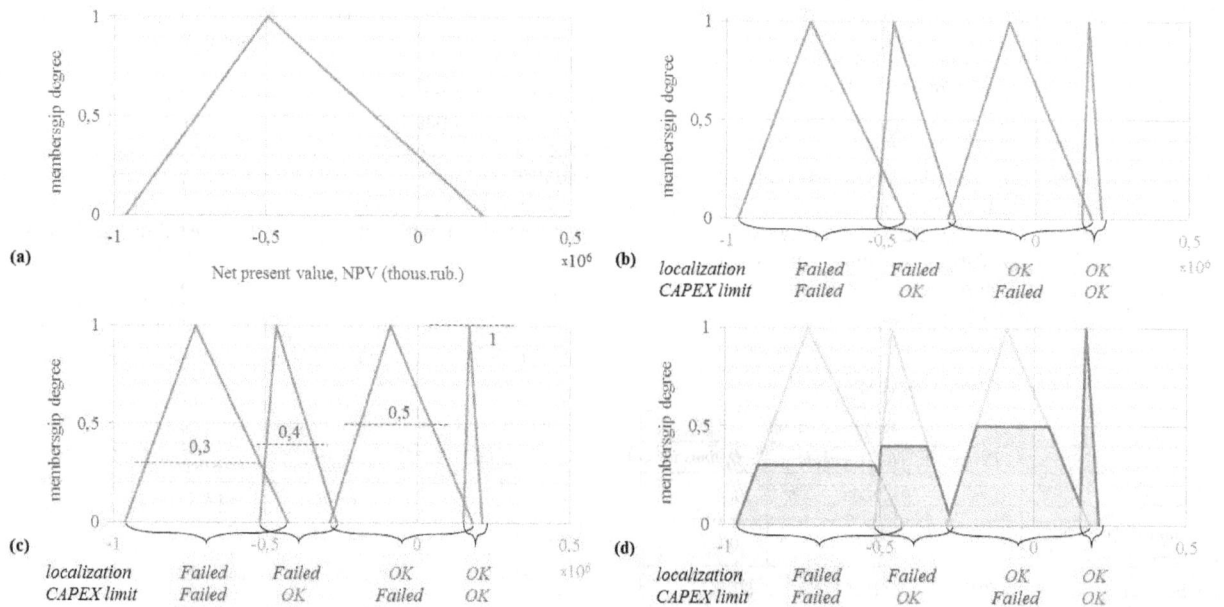

Fig. 3. Step-by-step illustration of converting triangular distribution to complex fuzzy pay-off representation: (a) constructing separate distribution for a case with high capacity factor (>75% of the target), (b) dividing it into four distributions in accordance with all combinations of fulfilling CapEx limit and localization requirement, (c) taking different alfa-cuts for each distribution, (d) taking union of resulting figures.

TABLE 3. FUZZY INFERENCE RULES FOR COMBINATIONS OF FACTORS

Factor		Alfa-cut level
Localization	CapEx limit	
Fulfilled	Fulfilled	1.0
Fulfilled	Failed	0.5
Failed	Fulfilled	0.4
Failed	Failed	0.3

electricity price and consumer price index remain as specified in Table 1, and capacity factor is equal to 75%, 97.5% and 120% respectively for three scenarios (since this is an illustration of the case when capacity factor is higher than 75% of the target).

To visually differentiate between these distributions, we cut them at different levels in accordance with fuzzy inference rules provided in Table 3 (Fig. 3 (c)). Thus, first to the right distribution that illustrates situation of both criteria fulfilled stays the same, next to it representing fulfilled localization and failed CapEx limit is cut at the membership degree equal to 0.5 etc. Finally, fuzzy union is taken of resulting figures forming complex payoff distribution (Fig. 3 (d)).

The same operations are performed for the two remaining cases with lower capacity factor. Resulting project payoff is shown in Fig. 5. Now a single graph illustrates all major combinations of uncertain factors, enabling us to trace the most important causal relationships from influential factors to the outcome. For instance, we can derive from the graph a conclusion that keeping CapEx within limit and fulfilled localization requirement, but having average capacity factor less than 50% of target (right purple peak with membership degree equal to 1.0) would generate about the same NPV range as failing first two constraints, but having higher capacity factor (left part of the orange distribution with membership degree equal to 0.3).

Another more important insight is that only capacity factor higher than 75% of the target in conjunction with fulfilled localization and CapEx within the limit would guarantee positive NPV. Moreover, project can sustain slight CapEx increase over the limit, but localization requirement and capacity factor level are crucial for its profitability.

Interestingly, resulting possibility distribution reflects

earlier obtained probability distribution in a greater extent than

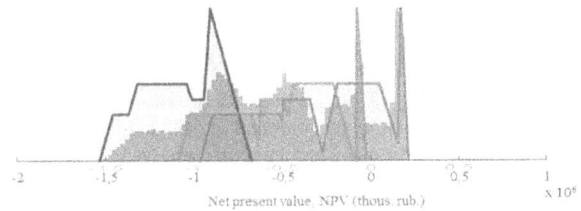

Fig. 4. Convergence of the probability and possibility distributions

the simple triangular distribution (Fig. 4). Reasons for the highly dissected shape of the probability distributions become clear. It results from the complex interaction of artificial effects of uncertain factors created by the supporting policy.

To summarize, breaking down complex influence of uncertain factors to their combinations and applying fuzzy inference rules create a possibility to display in a great detail not only the outcome of the project, but also its causality from uncertain factors.

IV. DISCUSSION AND CONCLUSIONS

The Datar-Mathews and the fuzzy pay-off method both exploit similar logic to real option valuation, but have different theoretical foundations, since DMM uses probabilistic distribution, while FPOM implies possibilistic one. Both techniques recognize the whole investment project as a real option and value it as an expected mean of all positive outcomes weighted on the success ratio.

In general, triangular possibility distribution can be a sufficient representative of the normal probability distribution without any harm to information content. However, in more complex cases, such as considered investment project benefiting from return-based legislative support, the simple triangular distribution appears to simplify the results substantially. In this case, both FPOM and DMM face the problem of linking influential factors with the outcome, since neither triangular distribution, nor dissected probability distribution can elucidate causal relationships.

However, the fuzzy set theory offers enough tools to tackle this problem. By dividing complex effects of uncertain factors into simple combinations of them and by applying fuzzy

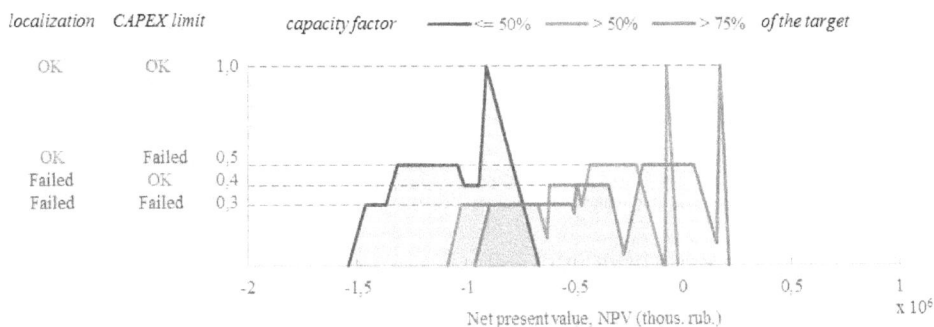

Fig. 5. Possibility distributions outlining all important combinations of uncertain factors.

inference rules to those combinations, insightful and self-sufficient results can be achieved. The aggregate possibility distribution is able to clearly demonstrate what outcomes result from what combination of factors, displaying both resulting outcomes and their links with interacting variables.

Combining fuzzy inference technique with the fuzzy pay-off method for complex investment cases can substantially facilitate and deepen investment analysis. Resulting distribution joins features of real option and sensitivity analyses becoming a unique and irreplaceable tool for investment decision-making.

Results of comparative analysis of DMM and FPOM signify consistence of the methods, since borders of possibility and probability distributions tally, although computed parameters, such as real option value, weighted NPV, standard deviation and success ratio do not match due to different theoretical foundations of two methods. However, it does not pose any problem for practical application as long as the only of two methods is used for analyzing and comparing different investment opportunities.

This paper contributes to existing literature on real option valuation by presenting comparative analysis of the two emerging methods. Such kind of comparison was not available before and would benefit further development of real option valuation methods. Adapting fuzzy inference to the fuzzy pay-off method represents a novel approach especially powerful for investment cases with complex interaction of uncertain factors. This modification of the FPOM would be a worthwhile adjustment to investment analysis for researchers and business analysts focused on such investment cases and for policymakers.

This study is limited to two specific methods, namely the Datar-Mathews method and the fuzzy pay-off method, leaving all other developments in real option valuation out of the focus. Their application is analyzed on the only investment case, however, generalizing the conclusions is eligible due to the common principles of investment analysis.

Scientific and business community would benefit from further research devoted to enhancement of investment and real option analysis techniques, for instance, suitable for assessing specific real options. Further extension of the fuzzy pay-off method with possibilistic theory tools seems fruitful direction of future research with great potential for decision-making.

ACKNOWLEDGMENT

The authors would like to acknowledge the support received by M. Kozlova from Fortum Foundation.

REFERENCES

[1] P.A. Ryan and G.P. Ryan, "Capital budgeting practices of the Fortune 1000: how have things changed," Journal of Business and Management, vol. 8, pp. 355-364, 2002.

[2] S. Block, "Are "real options" actually used in the real world?" The Engineering Economist, vol. 52, pp. 255-267, 2007.

[3] L. Trigeorgis, Real options: Managerial flexibility and strategy in resource allocation, MIT press, 1996.

[4] F. Black and M. Scholes, "The pricing of options and corporate liabilities," The Journal of Political Economy, pp. 637-654, 1973.

[5] J.C. Cox, S.A. Ross and M. Rubinstein, "Option pricing: A simplified approach," . Journal of Financial Economics, vol. 7, pp. 229-263, 1979.

[6] S. Mathews, V. Datar and B. Johnson, "A Practical Method for Valuing Real Options: The Boeing Approach," J.Appl.Corp.Finance, vol. 19, pp. 95-104, 2007.

[7] S. Mathews and J. Salmon, "Business engineering: a practical approach to valuing high-risk, highreturn projects using real options," Tutorials in Operations Research, 2007.

[8] V.T. Datar and S.H. Mathews, "European real options: An intuitive algorithm for the Black-Scholes formula," Journal of Applied Finance, vol. 14, pp. 45-51, 2004.

[9] M. Collan, R. Fullér and J. Mezei, "A fuzzy pay-off method for real option valuation," Journal of Applied Mathematics and Decision Sciences, vol. 2009, pp. 1-14, 2009.

[10] M. Collan, "The pay-off method: Re-inventing investment analysis," CreateSpace Inc., Charleston, 2012.

[11] J. Mezei, "A quantitative view on fuzzy numbers," Ph.D. dissertation, Abo Akademi University, Turku, Finland, pp. 191, 2011.

[12] C. Carlsson and R. Fullér, Possibility for decision: a possibilistic approach to real life decisions, Springer Science & Business Media, 2011.

[13] S. Johnson, T. Taylor and D. Ford, "Using system dynamics to extend real options use: Insights from the oil & gas industry," in International system dynamics conference, pp. 23-27, 2006.

[14] M. Collan, "Thoughts about selected models for the valuation of real options," Acta Universitatis Palackianae Olomucensis.Facultas Rerum Naturalium.Mathematica, vol. 50, pp. 5-12, 2011.

[15] C. Carlsson and R. Fullér, "On possibilistic mean value and variance of fuzzy numbers," Fuzzy Sets Syst., vol. 122, pp. 315-326, 2001.

[16] S. Mathews, "Valuing risky projects with real options," Research-Technology Management, vol. 52, pp. 32-41, 2009.

[17] M. Collan and J. Kinnunen, "A procedure for the rapid pre-acquisition screening of target companies using the pay-off method for real option valuation," Journal of Real Options and Strategy, vol. 4, pp. 117-141, 2011.

[18] M. Collan and M. Heikkilä, "Enhancing patent valuation with the pay-off method," Journal of Intellectual Property Rights, vol. 16, pp. 377-384, 2011.

[19] F. Hassanzadeh, M. Collan and M. Modarres, "A practical R&D selection model using fuzzy pay-off method," The International Journal of Advanced Manufacturing Technology, vol. 58, pp. 227-236, 01/01. 2012.

[20] M. Kozlova, "Analyzing the effects of the new renewable energy policy in Russia on investments into wind, solar and small hydro power," M.S. thesis, Lappeenranta University of Technology, Lappeenranta, Finland, pp. 104, 2015.

[21] Government of Russian Federation, "28 May 2013 Decree #449 on the mechanism of promoting the use of renewable energy in the wholesale market of electric energy and power," 2013.

[22] Government of Russian Federation, "28 May 2013 Resolution #861-r on amendments being made to Resolution #1-r 8.01.2009 on the main directions for the state policy to improve the energy efficiency of the electricity sector on the basis of renewable energy sources for the period up to 2020," 2013.

Valuing Managerial Cash-Flow Estimates with Market Related Timing Risk
Extended Abstract

Matt Davison
Department of Applied Mathematics
University of Western Ontario
London, Ontario, Canada
Email: `mdavison@uwo.ca`

Yuri Lawryshyn
Centre for the Management of Technology and Entrepreneurship
Department of Chemical Engineering and Applied Chemistry
University of Toronto
Toronto, Ontario, Canada
Email: `yuri.lawryshyn@utoronto.ca`

I. INTRODUCTION

Real option analysis (ROA) is recognized as a superior method to quantify the value of real-world investment opportunities where managerial flexibility can influence their worth, as compared to standard net present value (NPV) and discounted cash-flow (DCF) analysis. ROA stems from the work of Black and Scholes (1973) on financial option valuation. Myers (1977) recognized that both financial options and project decisions are exercised after uncertainties are resolved. Early techniques therefore applied the Black-Scholes equation directly to value put and call options on tangible assets (see, for example, Brennan and Schwartz (1985)). Since then, ROA has gained significant attention in academic and business publications, as well as textbooks (Copeland and Tufano (2004), Trigeorgis (1996)).

While a number of practical and theoretical approaches for real option valuation have been proposed in the literature, industry's adoption of real option valuation is limited, primarily due to the inherent complexity of the models (Block (2007)). A number of leading practical approaches, some of which have been embraced by industry, lack financial rigor, while many theoretical approaches are not practically implementable. Previously, we developed a real options analysis framework where we assumed that future cash-flow estimates are provided by the manager in the form of a probability density function (PDF) at each time period (Jaimungal and Lawryshyn (2015)). As was presented, the PDF can simply be triangular (representing typical, optimistic and pessimistic scenarios), normal, log-normal, or any other continuous density. Second, we assumed that there exists a *market sector indicator* that uniquely determines the cash-flow for each time period and that this indicator is a Markov process. The market sector indicator can be thought of as market size or other such value. Third, we assumed that there exists a tradable asset whose returns are correlated to the market sector indicator.

While this assumption may seem somewhat restrictive, it is likely that in many market sectors it is possible to identify some form of market sector indicator for which historical data exists and whose correlation to a traded asset/index could readily be determined. One of the key ingredients of our original approach is that the process for the market sector indicator determines the managerial estimated cash-flows, thus ensuring that the cash-flows from one time period to the next are consistently correlated. A second key ingredient is that an appropriate risk-neutral measure is introduced through the minimal martingale measure (MMM) (Föllmer and Schweizer (1991)), thus ensuring consistency with financial theory in dealing with market and private risk, and eliminating the need for subjective estimates of the appropriate discount factor typically required in a discounted cash-flow (DCF) calculation. We then expanded our methodology to be able to account for managerial risk aversion. Furthermore, we developed an analytical approach for the case where the cash-flows are assumed to be normally distributed (Lawryshyn (2013)).

After using our method in a few practical settings where we valued early stage projects, we realized that a key ingredient was missing in much of the real options approaches, including ours – that of timing risk. In this work we develop a framework that provides a practical way to deal with timing risk. Furthermore, we allow the timing risk to be (partially) correlated to the market.

II. METHODOLOGY

A key assumption of many real options approaches (Copeland and Antikarov (2001), Datar and Mathews (2004) and Collan, Fullér, and Mezei (2009)), is that the risk profile of the project is reflected in the distribution of uncertainty provided by managerial cash-flow estimates. In Jaimungal and Lawryshyn (2010), we introduced a "Matching Method", where, as mentioned above, we assumed that there exists a *market sector indicator* Markov process that ultimately drives

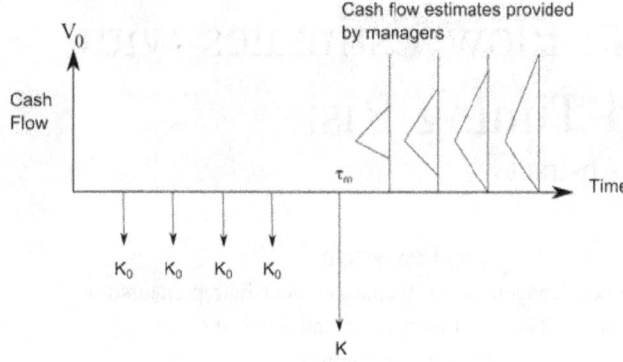

Fig. 1. Cash-flow scenario. The timing, τ_m, is uncertain.

the managerial-supplied cash-flow estimates. The value of the method is the riskiness of the cash-flows are inherently accounted for by the managerial supplied distribution. A broader distribution necessarily implies a more risky cash-flow. As well, the method properly accounts for idiosyncratic and systematic risk (for full details of our methodology we refer the reader to Jaimungal and Lawryshyn (2015)). As we develop our method here, we set out two main objectives: 1) that the model be consistent with financial theory, and 2) that the methodology is easily adapted to managerial estimates.

A depiction of the project cash-flow scenario is provided in Figure 1. The during development, regular outlays of cash will be required for the project and these are depicted as K_0 [1]. At some point τ_m the project will be ready for the market, at which point a significant investment K will be required after which cash-flows generated through revenue and operations are expected to be received. These cash-flows are uncertain and are estimated by managers. As discussed in Jaimungal and Lawryshyn (2015) the distribution of the cash-flow estimates can take any form, however, for practical reasons, in this formulation, we assume them to have a triangular density representing low, medium and high cash-flow estimates. The cash-flows are assumed to occur at times T_k, $k = 1, 2, ..., n$, where n is the number of cash-flows. In the present formulation, we assume these cash-flows are not dependent on τ_m, however, this assumption can be easily relaxed and in fact, using either fuzzy set theory or probabilistic methods, it is possible to distort these cash-flows appropriately.

To allow for proper valuation of both systematic and idiosyncratic risk, we assume there exists a traded index index that follows geometric Brownian motion (GBM),

$$\frac{dI_t}{I_t} = \mu dt + \sigma dB_t, \quad (1)$$

[1]We note that in the current formulation we have assumed these to be equivalent, however in practice this does not have to be the case.

where B_t is a standard Brownian motion under the real-world measure $\mathbb{P}$. Following Jaimungal and Lawryshyn (2015) we assume there exists a market sector indicator that is partially correlated to the traded index and we assume it has a standard Brownian motion,

$$dS_t = \rho_S dB_t + \sqrt{1 - \rho_S^2} dW_t^S, \quad (2)$$

where W_t^S is a standard Brownian motion under the real-world measure $\mathbb{P}$ independent from B_t, and ρ_S is a constant ($-1 \leq \rho_S \leq 1$). Next, we introduce a collection of functions $\varphi_k(S_t)$ such that at each T_k, $S_k = \varphi_k(S_{T_k})$. Furthermore, at each cash-flow date T_k we match the the distribution S_k to the cash-flow distribution supplied by the manager $F^*(x)$. Thus, we require

$$\mathbb{P}(S_T < x) = F^*(x). \quad (3)$$

In our previous work (Jaimungal and Lawryshyn (2010)) it was shown that $\varphi_k(S_t)$ is determined as follows

$$\varphi_k(x) = F^{*-1}\left(\Phi\left(\frac{x}{\sqrt{T_k}}\right)\right), \quad (4)$$

where $\Phi(\bullet)$ is the standard normal distribution. We now have a very simple expression for φ which makes the valuation of risky cash-flows very simple.

As discussed in Jaimungal and Lawryshyn (2010), the real-world pricing measure should not be used, and instead, we propose the risk-neutral measure $\mathbb{Q}$, corresponding to a variance minimizing hedge. Under this risk-neutral measure, we have the following dynamics

$$\frac{dI_t}{I_t} = r\,dt + \sigma\,d\widehat{B}_t, \quad (5)$$

$$dS_t = \nu_S\,dt + \rho_S\,d\widehat{B}_t + \sqrt{1 - \rho_S^2}\,d\widehat{W}_t^S, \quad (6)$$

where $\widehat{B}_t$ and $\widehat{W}_t^S$ are standard uncorrelated Brownian motions under the risk-neutral measure $\mathbb{Q}$ and the risk-neutral drift of the indicator is

$$\nu_S = -\rho_S \frac{\mu - r}{\sigma}. \quad (7)$$

We emphasize that the drift of the indicator is precisely the CAPM drift of an asset correlated to the market index and is a reflection of a deeper connection between the MMM and the CAPM as demonstrated in (Cerny 1999). Given this connection, our reliance on parameter estimation is similar to those invoked by standard DCF analysis when the weighted average cost of capital (WACC) is used to discount cash-flows and the cost of equity is estimated using CAPM. In DCF analysis the CAPM drift is, however, estimated based on the company's beta, while in our approach, the CAPM drift derives from historical estimates of the sector indicator and traded index dynamics. Furthermore, the *riskiness* of the project is appropriately captured by the distribution of the cash-flows.

Consequently, our approach is more robust. Given the risk measure $\mathbb{Q}$, the values of the cash-flows can now be computed; i.e. at time τ_m the cash-flows can be valued as

$$V_{\tau_m}^{CF}(S_{\tau_m}) = \sum_{k=1}^{n} e^{-r(T_k - \tau_m)} \mathbb{E}^{\mathbb{Q}} \left[\varphi_k(S_{T_k}) | S_{\tau_m} \right], \quad (8)$$

and the option value accounting for investment K just before time τ_m as

$$V_{\tau_m^-}^{RO}(S_{\tau_m}) = \left(V_{\tau_m}^{CF}(S_{\tau_m}) - K \right)_+. \quad (9)$$

Applying the discounted Feynman-Kac theorem, the value of the cash-flows for $t \in [\tau_m, T_n]$ can be determined using the PDE

$$rV = \frac{\partial V}{\partial t} + \nu_S \frac{\partial V}{\partial s} + \frac{1}{2} \frac{\partial^2 V}{\partial s^2}, \quad (10)$$

where at each $t = T_k^+$ we have $V_{T_k^+}(S_{T_k}) = V_{T_k}(S_{T_k}) + \varphi_k(S_{T_k})$. The finite difference method used to solve equation (10) where in the implementation we assumed $\frac{\partial V}{\partial s}$ is constant as $s \to \pm\infty$ and at each time step negative values were set to zero to account for an American style option where the project would be abandoned as soon as it no longer has value.

As mentioned, a key aspect of the formulation presented here is the timing risk associated with when the technological development of the project will be ready for revenue generation. As such, we ask the managers to provide a distribution estimate for τ_m. Now, we introduce as second Brownian motion with drift μ_τ,

$$dG_t = \mu_\tau dt + \rho_\tau dB_t + \sqrt{1 - \rho_\tau^2} dW_t^\tau, \quad (11)$$

where, similar to the cash-flow driver process, W_t^τ is another standard Brownian motion under the real-world measure $\mathbb{P}$ independent from B_t and W_t^S, and ρ_τ is a constant ($-1 \leq \rho_\tau \leq 1$). Under the risk-neutral measure the process in equation (11) becomes

$$d\widehat{G}_t = \nu_\tau dt + \rho_\tau d\widehat{B}_t + \sqrt{1 - \rho_\tau^2} d\widehat{W}_t^\tau, \quad (12)$$

where $\widehat{W}_t^\tau$ is another standard uncorrelated Brownian motion under the risk-neutral measure $\mathbb{Q}$ and the risk-neutral drift is

$$\nu_\tau = \mu_\tau - \rho_\tau \frac{\mu - r}{\sigma}. \quad (13)$$

By choosing a boundary at at some value a we can calculate the distribution of the hitting time such that $\mathbb{P}(\tau_m \leq t)$, where $\tau_m = \min(t \geq 0, G_t = a)$, as

$$F_{\tau_m}(t) = e^{2\mu_\tau a} \Phi\left(\frac{-a - \mu_\tau t}{\sqrt{t}} \right) + 1 - \Phi\left(\frac{a - \mu_\tau t}{\sqrt{t}} \right). \quad (14)$$

We use equation (14) to match the managerial estimated distribution for τ_m to determine appropriate values for a and μ_τ and constrain $a > 0$.

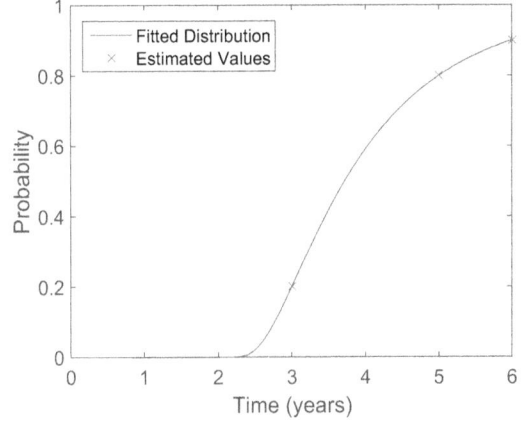

Fig. 2. Fitted distribution for τ_m.

Applying the Feynman-Kac theorem, the value of the project $V = V_t(s, g)$ can be determined using the PDE

$$rV = \frac{\partial V}{\partial t} + \nu_S \frac{\partial V}{\partial s} + \nu_\tau \frac{\partial V}{\partial g} + \frac{1}{2} \frac{\partial^2 V}{\partial s^2} + \frac{1}{2} \frac{\partial^2 V}{\partial g^2} + \frac{\partial^2 V}{\partial s \partial g}, \quad (15)$$

for $t \in [t_0, t_{max}]$ where t_0 and t_{max} are the minimum and maximum times, as specified by the managers, for which the project is expected to be marketed; i.e. $\tau_m \in [t_0, t_{max}]$. For all $t \in [t_0, t_{max}]$ we have $V_t(S_t, a) = V_t^{RO}(S_t)$ and, as before, we assume $\frac{\partial V_t(s,g)}{\partial s}$ is constant as $s \to \pm\infty$. For all $t \in [t_0, t_{max})$ we assume $\frac{\partial V_t(s,g)}{\partial g}$ is constant as $g \to -\infty$. At $t = t_{max}$ we set $V_{t_{max}}(s, g) = 0, \forall s$ and $g < a$. Since the project cannot achieve market launch before t_0, equation (10) is implemented for all $t \in [0, t_0)$. To account for ongoing development costs K_0 at each $t_j = 1, 2, ..., t_{max}$ we make the adjustment $V_{t_j^+}(s, g) = V_{t_j}(s, g) - K_0$. As above, an American option formulation was implemented to account for the fact that the project would be abandoned as soon as it had no value.

III. RESULTS

Here we provide a practical implementation of the methodology. We assume that a company is interested in investing in an early stage R&D project. The managers estimate that technology could be ready for market launch as early as 2 years from now, but if not launched within 6 years, it will be abandoned. Specifically, the managers estimate a 20% of market launch by year 3, 80% by year 5 and a 10% chance of no launch within the 6 years. The fitted distribution using equation (14) is plotted in Figure 2 and the fitted parameters were $a = 2.081$ and $\mu_\tau = 0.9782$.

The market parameters are assumed to be as follows:

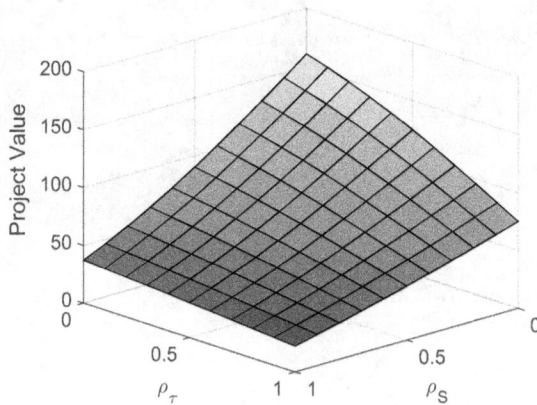

Fig. 3. Project value as a function of ρ_S and ρ_τ.

- Risk-free rate: $r = 3\%$
- Expected market growth: $\mu = 10\%$
- Market volatility: $\sigma = 10\%$.

Managers have estimated the cash-flows to be as depicted in Table I and the correlation of the cash-flows to the traded index are estimated to be 0.5. The cost to enter the market for the technology K was estimated to be $50 million and year per-market expenditures were estimated to be $5 million. The value of the project was determined to be $71.2 million for the case where the timing had a 0.5 correlation to the market index. Figure 3 plots the project value as a function of both ρ_S and ρ_τ. As can be seen from the figure, the project value is more sensitive to ρ_S however, the timing estimates have a significant impact on the overall project value.

TABLE I
MANAGERIAL SUPPLIED CASH-FLOWS (MILLIONS $).

	$\tau_m + 1$	$\tau_m + 2$	$\tau_m + 3$	$\tau_m + 4$	$\tau_m + 5$	$\tau_m + 6$
Low	10	20	20	10	10	5
Medium	30	40	50	60	60	50
High	50	70	100	120	130	120

REFERENCES

Black, F. and M. Scholes (1973). The pricing of options and corporate liabilities. *Journal of Political Economy 81*, 637–659.

Block, S. (2007). Are real options actually used in the real world? *Engineering Economist 52*(3), 255–267.

Brennan, M. J. and S. Schwartz (1985). Evaluating natural resource investments. *Journal of Business 58*(2), 135–157.

Cerny, A. (1999). Minimal martingale measure, capm, and representative agent pricing in incomplete markets. Technical report, Cass Business School. Available at SSRN: http://ssrn.com/abstract=851188.

Collan, M., R. Fullér, and J. Mezei (2009). A fuzzy pay-off method for real option valuation. *Journal of Applied Mathematics and Decision Sciences*, 1–14.

Copeland, T. and V. Antikarov (2001). *Real Options: A Practitioner's Guide*. W. W. Norton and Company.

Copeland, T. and P. Tufano (2004, March). A real-world way to manage real options. *Harvard Business Review 82*(3), 90–99.

Datar, V. and S. Mathews (2004). European real options: An intuitive algorithm for the black- scholes formula. *Journal of Applied Finance 14*(1), 45–51.

Föllmer, H. and M. Schweizer (1991). *Applied Stochastic Analysis : Stochastics Monographs*, Chapter Hedging of contingent claims under incomplete information, pp. 389–414. Gordon and Breach, London.

Jaimungal, S. and Y. A. Lawryshyn (2010). Incorporating managerial information into real option valuation. *Avaiable at SSRN: http://ssrn.com/abstract=1730355*.

Jaimungal, S. and Y. A. Lawryshyn (2015). *Incorporating Managerial Information into Real Option Valuation*. Fields Volume on Commodities, Energy, and Environmental Finance. Forthcoming.

Lawryshyn, Y. A. (2013, July). A closed-form model for valuing real options using managerial cash-flow estimates. In *Proceedings of the Real Options Conference*.

Myers, S. (1977). Determinants of corporate borrowing. *Journal of Financial Economics 5*, 147–175.

Trigeorgis, L. (1996). *Real Options: Managerial Flexibility and Strategy in Resource Allocation*. Cambridge, MA: The MIT Press.

R&D alliances timing under uncertainty: from theory toward experiments

Azzurra Morreale
Department of Economics and Management
University of Trento
Trento, Italy
azzurra.morreale@unipa.it

Liam Rose
Department of Economics
University of California, Santa Cruz
Santa Cruz, USA
lrose1@ucsc.edu

Giovanna Lo Nigro
DICGIM
University of Palermo
Palermo, Italy
giovanna.lonigro@unipa.it

Abstract— There is a growing awareness that managers have cognitive biases when making investments decisions under uncertainty. There is evidence of deviation from the predictions derived using normative models, such as real options models. The proposed research sheds light on the importance of integrating normative models with experimental methods in order to predict and explain such cognitive limitations. To this aim, starting from a real options model dealing with alliance timing decisions, we propose a simple design of an experiment, that can been used to test some of the fundamental insights of real options theory in the context of R&D alliances.

Keywords— Real options; R&D alliances; behavioural decision theory.

I. INTRODUCTION

It is widely accepted that many of the investments decisions facing with uncertainty can be characterized as real options problems [1,2]. Consequently, the development of normative techniques to evaluate real options investments has gained increased attention. As a matter of fact, real options analysis (ROA) has been recognized as a tool to evaluate investments that involve a significant amount of uncertainty [3]. Recently ROA has been using also to evaluate R&D alliances established between firms [4,5,6,7,8]. These agreements not only generate stochastic benefits (uncertainty) but also bring sunk costs (irreversibility). In addition, a key element in these agreements is flexibility: firms have the opportunity, but not the obligation to sign an alliance, or sometimes the right to renew an existing one. In other words they can wait to form an alliance when more information is available. Therefore, analyzing R&D alliances in a real options framework can precisely capture these important three aspects [9].

Despite the normative work on real option valuation, only recently some researches have called for studying behavioural

aspects of managing real options [2]. These studies highlight that individuals exhibit systematic deviations from the predictions derived using normative models [10].

This research attempts to extend the boundaries of real options analysis to environments where people have biases in their decision-making, especially in the context of R&D alliances and merger and acquisitions. Consistent with neo-classical rational theory, prior studies show that mergers are driven by rational expectations of growth options, synergies or reallocation of assets in a response to industry shocks. The rational view also includes real options models, where decisions such as acquisitions waves for example are driven by growth opportunities [11]. However, contrary to rational theory, decision makers may act irrationally when making acquisition choices under uncertainty [12,13, 23]. Investors' exuberance, positive sentiments of boards as well as cognitive biases - such as risk aversion - influence companies' acquisition behaviour under uncertainty. To use Smit and Lovallo's [13] words, "acquisition strategy is vulnerable to the way managers perceive risk and losses, judgment biases in their strategy, the bidding behaviour of rivals and mispricing in financial markets".

The controlled environment of a laboratory setting may allow us to take these important aspects into consideration and to get a better idea about how subjects make risky decisions in the particular context of R&D alliances and mergers and acquisitions.

With this aim, starting from a real options model available in literature (developed by Lo Nigro et al. [8]) that deals with R&D alliance timing decisions in a stochastic environment, we propose a design of experiment that can be used to test if people make decisions conforming to the normative model. We also conducted a pilot that illustrates how the design could be implemented.

The remainder of the paper is organized as follows. In the next section we provide an overview of the experimental methodology. Both advantages and possible shortcomings are discussed. In section III we discuss the relevant literature. In section IV we present the theoretical model, while in section V we describe the design of the experiment conducted. In section 6, conclusions are drawn and further developments are anticipated.

II. THE EXPERIMENTAL METHODOLOGY: AN OVERVIEW

The use of laboratory experiments has grown significantly over the last few decades in economics and in finance as well as in other several fields. In fact, there are numerous advantages in adopting such an approach [14, 15, 16]. First of all, experimental economics allow for a controlled environment where data are generated. By making *ceteris paribus* changes in the exogenous variables, the researcher can easily evaluate and compare alternative theories. Second, data are replicable. Whereas it could be very difficult to replicate a field data set, it is easier to reproduce the experiment and replicate the results. In addition, many variables cannot be observed in the field, but they can be observed in the laboratory [14]. It follows that the laboratory approach sometimes could be the only way to test a theory, such as the real options theory. As Yavas and Sirmanas [14] point out, empirical testing of real options has been scarce. This is primarily due to the problems that researchers face in obtaining "key variables" in real options, i.e. reliable data on such components of the real options approach as the current and future value of the underlying asset and the variability of value [14,16]. As a matter of fact, such information is very difficult to estimate from the field data. Conversely, such data can be easily generated in a laboratory experiment. In addition, even if data are available, very often they are not available in the form that would respect the assumptions of the theoretical models. This is particularly true in individual choice problems and game theoretical analysis [14].

Despite these undisputed advantages, perhaps the most fundamental question in experimental economics is whether findings from the laboratory are generalizable outside of the laboratory (external validity). This consideration calls for the well-known tension between internal and external validity of the experimental methodology. Internal validity very often requires abstraction and simplification of theory in order to make the research more tractable. However, as both abstraction and simplification increase, the external validity decreases [15]. On the other hand, most of the economic models are unrealistic, e.g. they leave out many aspect of the reality. However the simplicity of a model very often is an advantage because it enhances our understanding of the interaction of relevant variables. Similar considerations also hold for a laboratory experiment. At a minimum, laboratory experiments can provide a crucial first understanding of a theory and can suggest underlying mechanisms that might be at work when certain data patterns are observed. A metaphor provided by Levitt and List [16] illustrates this concept. " ..experimenters are like aerodynamicists who use wind tunnels to test models of proposed aircraft, helicopters, cars, and trains. The wind tunnel provides the engineer with valuable data on scale models much like the lab provides economists with important insights on an economic phenomenon"[16]. Moreover, in cases where collection of field data is expensive, an experimental approach can be used as a less costly alternative to generating the desired data [14]. Through rigorous testing and re-testing, it is possible to obtain important insights on an economic phenomenon. Then, the researcher can investigate more in details the phenomenon in the field, at a more expansive cost.

III. RELATED LITERATURE

As Moel and Tufano [17] note, " empirical research on real options has lagged considerably behind the conceptual and theoretical contribution". In the last decade, researchers have been using laboratory experiments to study real option theory empirically.

In Miller and Shapira's [2] work, decision makers are presented with simple binary lotteries and asked to specify the price for selling or buying a call or a put option for the gambles. The results show that the value of the price specified for selling and buying the derivate do not coincide, suggesting inadequacy with the normative model's descriptive power [10]. Yavas and Sirmanas [14] investigate the option "wait and see" in the laboratory. The results of their experiments highlight that fundamental insights of real options theory are not so evident to individual investors. As a matter of fact, the majority of subjects tend to invest too early compared to the optimal timing suggested by the theoretical model and thus fail to realize the benefits of waiting. Close to the spirit of this paper, Oprea et al. [18] investigate behaviour in uncertain investment opportunities governed by Brownian motion. Their results indicate that people can closely approximate optimal exercise of wait options if they have decent chance to learn from personal experience [18]. In fact, while at the beginning investors tend to exercise the option prematurely, over time their average behaviour converges close to the optimum. In Murphy and Knaus [10] work, a decision maker must choose how much to invest in a risky environment that evolves over time. Their experimental results contrast predictions from theory.

These findings suggest innate behavioural tendencies that are contrary to the normative dictates as most of the above works highlights that people have biases in their decision-making. However, these studies have investigated human choice behaviour in investment decisions under uncertainty, while our research deals with human choice behaviour in alliance decisions under uncertainty. In addition, while in these previous studies subjects made choices where a simple and discrete (traditionally binomial) stochastic model that governs cash flows was considered, we propose a design where a more realistic and continuous stochastic model that governs cash flows is considered, such that subjects are confronted with multiple outcomes.

IV. THE THEORETICAL MODEL (MONOPOLY CASE)

A. Problem description

As noted previously, we refer to a theoretical model developed by Lo Nigro et al. [8] who introduced and analyzed the effect of competition in biotechnology industry by modeling the decisions of whether and when ally with a pharmaceutical company through a real options game.

To better understand the design of the experiment we propose, let us briefly recall the theoretical model in the monopoly case. Consider a firm, named firm A, which is working on a research and development (R&D) project. Also, consider a simple setup in which there are two stages of the development process. The first stage, named R&D stage, includes the research phases as well as the development phase. In the second and final stage the project is approaching commercialization. The market value of the project is uncertain and it can change during the first stage. In particular, let the market value projection over time be represented by a non-negative random process V(t). In our analysis we make the additional assumption that V(t) follows a geometric Brownian motion (GBM).

At each stage, the firm will have the option to form an alliance with firm B. Firm A can also choose to forgo the alliance and choose to enter the market alone. The sequence of the game is as follows. At the beginning of the first stage (t=0), firm A's project value is given by V_0. Firm B offers an alliance contract to Firm A consisting of an ex-ante payment P_1 and percentage of royalties retained by firm A equal to $1-\alpha_1$, $0<\alpha_1<1$. If firm A rejects the offer, the decision game is repeated. In the second stage (t=1, with T the length of the first stage), Firm B offers a different alliance contract consisting of an ex-ante payment P_2 and a percentage of royalties equal to $1-\alpha_2$, $0<\alpha_2<1$. If firm A rejects this offer, the firm proceeds to the final market unassisted.

In each stage i, an investment payment I_i must be made. If an alliance is formed at stage i, the size of the project's market increases relative to the case of no alliance by an amplification factor $\delta > 1$. This factor reflects the value added to the project by the synergies derived from the alliance. In order to keep the model as simple as possible, we assume royalty payments are the same regardless of when alliance was formed (i.e. $\alpha_1 = \alpha_2 = \alpha$). Thus, if an alliance is signed, the value of the project will be multiplied by K, with K equal to $\delta(1-\alpha)$.

Fig. 1 depicts the extensive form of the tree. Note that $C(S;X)$ is the value of the call option (computed through Black and Sholes formula (Black and Sholes, [19]) with underlying S and exercise price X.

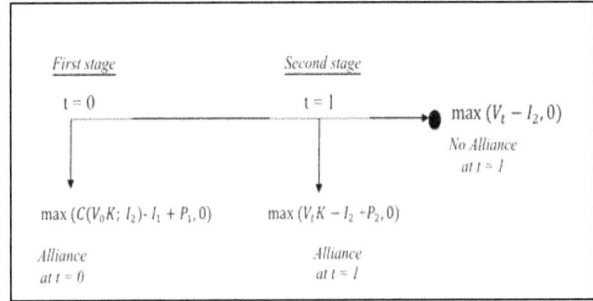

Fig. 1. Extensive form of the tree

The game can be solved via backward induction procedure. Therefore, we start from the second stage where firm A has to decide if ally or not with firm B and go back to the first stage. It is straightforward to see that we can obtain three possible scenarios (j) of *equilibrium* for the game. These are (see TABLE I): Firm A's alliance at stage 1 (equilibrium Q1), Firm A's alliance at stage 2 (Q2), and no Firm A's alliance (Q3).

TABLE I. SCENARIOS OF EQUILIBRIUM (MONOPOLY CASE)

$Q_{j=1,2,3}$	Q_1	Q_2	Q_3
Firm A	Alliance at first stage with Firm B	Alliance at second stage with Firm B	No alliance

B. Computing payoffs

As mentioned, the pharmaceutical process is split in two stages: the R&D stage and the commercialization stage, with the market value of the project that is uncertain and able to change during the first stage. As a consequence, the R&D stage is an option for the second and final stage. This means that the process can been seen as a 1-fold option, i.e. a simple option. Accordingly, we can model it with the Black and Sholes approach, which ensures the flexibility offered by the option to decide further investments when more information is available. Adopting such an approach means assuming that the value of the project V_0 at the beginning of the first stage follows a geometric Brownian motion and as such this value, at maturity T (i.e. at the end of the first stage or alternatively at the beginning of the second stage), is a known realization from a lognormal distribution. Then, the second stage payoffs are function of the known realization of the value of the project at maturity (V_T). At the beginning of the second stage, uncertainty is solved and the realization of the underlying is known (see Fig. 2, where a possible realization at maturity is indicated). In other words, after the R&D stage, the company has more information about the value of cash flows coming from commercialization.

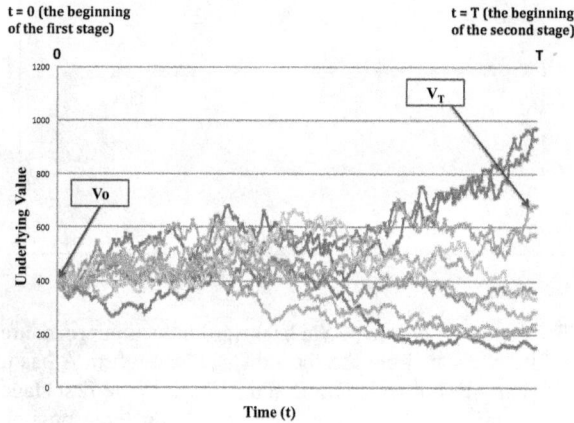

Fig. 2. Underying value representation (Considering 10 replications) from the beginning to the end of the first stage

In this way, the payoffs in the first stage are computed as call European options $C(S;X)$ in order to take into account uncertainty in this stage (please refer to TABLE II).

TABLE II.   ELEMENTS NECESSARY TO COMPUTE FIRST STAGE PAYOFFS

$Q_{j=1,2,3}$	Q_1	Q_2	Q_3
S^j	C^1	C^2	C^3
Underlying (S^j)	KV_0	$KV_0 + E(P_2)$	V_0
Exercise price (X^j)	I_2	I_2	I_2
Net Invest. (t=0)	$I_1 - P_1$	I_1	I_1

Conversely, the simple NPV is used to compute the second stage payoffs (please refer to TABLE III).

TABLE III.   ELEMENTS NECESSARY TO COMPUTE SECOND STAGE PAYOFFS

$Q_{j=2,3}$	Q_2	Q_3
Project Value V^j	KV_T	V_T
Net Invest. (t=0)	$I_2 - P_2$	I_2

In particular, at the beginning of the second stage (i.e. at t=1) the value of the project V(T), is log-normally distributed with mean and variance equal respectively to:

$$E[V(T)]=V_0 e^{rT} \tag{1}$$

$$Var[V(T)]=V^2_0 e^{2rT}(e^{s2T}-1) \tag{2}$$

Where s is the volatility of V_0; and r is the risk-free interest rate.

If an alliance is formed, the value of the project will be $V_0 K$, where V_0 follows a Geometric Brownian Motion as above. In this case, the value of the project VK(T) at t=1, is log-normally distributed with mean and variance equal respectively to:

$$E[VK(T)]=V_0 K e^{rT} \tag{3}$$

$$Var[VK(T)]=V^2_0 K^2 e^{2rT}(e^{s2T}-1) \tag{4}$$

Since the payments in the second stage are linear function of the value of the project, if Firm A decides to wait and sign an alliance at the second stage, she will receive a P_2, which is a realization from a log-normal distribution with mean and variance equal to:

$$E[VP_2(T)]=V_0(1-K)e^{rT} \tag{5}$$

$$Var[VP_2 (T)]=V^2_0 (1-K)^2 e^{2rT}(e^{s2T}-1) \tag{6}$$

Conversely, if firm A signs an alliance at the first stage, she will receive a sure payment P_1 computed as a difference of two calls options[1].

Under this setting, we find the threshold payments, i.e., P_1 and $E(P_2)$, that determine the possible scenarios of equilibrium (TABLE IV).

TABLE IV.   THRESHOLD PAYMENTS (P_1 AND $E(P_2)$) AND POSSIBLE SCENARIOS OF EQUILIBRIUM IN THE MONOPOLY CASE

		P_1	
		Low	High
$E(P_2)$	Low	$E(P_2)<V^3 - V^2$	$P_1 < C^3 - C^1$ **No Alliance**	$P_1 > C^3 - C^1$ **Firm A first stage**
	High	$E(P_2)>V^3 - V^2$	$P_1 < C^2 - C^1$ **Firm A second stage**	$P_1 > C^2 - C^1$ **Firm A first stage**

Specifically, the normative model suggests that, if firm B does not offer a considerable amount of payment in the initial stage, i.e., P_1 low, firm A firm might profit more from waiting until the second stage to possibly obtain better payment conditions. In the second stage, in fact, firm A will ally with firm B only under favorable expected payment conditions, i.e., high values of $E(P_2)$. Otherwise, firm A should continue the R&D process on her own. Interestingly, if, in the first stage, the payment conditions are sufficiently high, firm A will sign an early alliance independently of any expected value of P_2.

To better visualize these results and provide a practical application of the relative insights, we complement the analytical derivation with a numerical analysis, assuming high values of $E(P_2)$. Given this assumption, depending on the value assumed by P_1, the equilibrium suggested by the model would be an alliance at the first or at the second stage.

---

[1] Readers can refer to Lo Nigro et al. [8] for an exhaustive description of the model.

Consider the following set of parameters: $V_0 = \$400$, s = 30%, r = 5%, $I_1 = \$75$, $I_2 = \$180$; T=2, δ (2.2). Fig. 3 identifies the region of alliance as a function of P_1 and α. Therefore, assuming a payment P_1 equal to 17.8 and α = 0.6, the theoretical equilibrium is the alliance at the second stage.

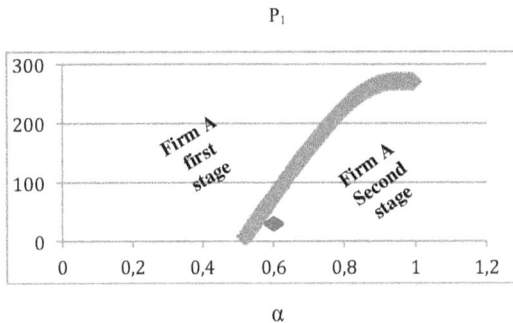

Fig. 3. P_1 threshold ($P_1 = C^2 - C^1$) when $E(P_2)$ is high

When "waiting" is the optimal strategy, do investors postpone the alliance decision until uncertainty is resolved (i.e. in the second stage)? In other words do people, on average, make decisions conforming to the theoretical model? One factor that influences this kind of decision is risk-aversion. Consider $P_1 = C^2 - C^1$, i.e. equal to the threshold payment. In such a case according to the normative model, people should be indifferent between signing an alliance at the first stage rather than at the second stage. However a more risk-averse individual will be more likely to choose the sure payment. Do people prefer a sure payment at the first stage upon a risky payment at the second stage that could be either higher or lower? We designed an experiment that explicitly takes into account this important aspect.

V.   DESIGN OF EXPERIMENT

We provided people with 20 choices between a sure outcome and a risky one.

In particular, we chose input parameters in order to obtain a high value of $E(P_2)$ and $P_1 = C^2 - C^1$. Given our assumptions about the diffusion process of $V(t)$, the decision maker (assuming she is playing the role of firm A) has to choose between a sure payment if she decides to ally at the first stage and a risky payment from a continuous distribution - in particular lognormal distribution - if she decides to ally in the second stage. Furthermore we chose input values in order to have P_1 almost equal to the discounted $E(P_2)$, so that people made a choice between a sure outcome and a risky one with the same expected value (TABLE V shows different values of the sure payment (P_1) and the expected value of the risky payment (P_2))[2].

Studying such a situation would allow us to test an important factor that can influences people in making alliance decisions, i.e. their risk preferences. Works on risk attitudes assume risk aversion [2]. "The preference for the sure gain is an instance of risk aversion. In general, a preference for a sure outcome over a gamble that has higher or equal expectation is called risk aversion, and the rejection of a sure thing in favor of a gamble of lower or equal expectation is called risk seeking" [20]. Evidence suggests that the same person may behave as risk averse and risk seeking in different situations [21]. In particular, when dealing with risky alternatives with gains as possible outcomes, people appear risk averse; when dealing with risky alternatives with possible loss outcomes, people tend to be risk seeking [2,20]. It follows that whether choices are framed as gains or losses is crucial to evaluate individuals' risk preference. In our case, people will choose between a sure payoff and gains as possible outcomes. Therefore, we can test the risk-aversion hypothesis. As a matter of fact, they will choose between a positive sure payment P_1 and a risky positive payment P_2, which is lognormally distributed as previously shown. Therefore, as said earlier, a more risk-averse individual will be more likely to choose the sure payment.

TABLE V.   DIFFERENT VALUES OF THE SURE PAYMENT (P_1) AND THE EXPECTED VALUE OF THE RISKY PAYMENT (P_2) AT T=0, WHEN I_2=18; K= 0,88; S =0.4; R = 0.05 AND V_0 VARIES FROM 30 TO 41.

P_1 CERTAIN PAYOFF (B&S)	DISCOUNTED $E(P_2)$
17.84	17.86
17.03	17.03
15.88	16.36
15.6	15.6
14.35	14.42
13.33	13.12
13.22	13.13
12.12	11.99
10.92	10.92
10.07	9.98
9.40	9.15
8.69	8.30
7.92	7.15
7.70	6.79
26.72	26.75
31.28	31.29
36.23	36.23
35.68	35.69
36.62	36.80
18.24	17.46

A. Implementation

We conducted a pilot with nine students from University of California Santa Cruz.

The experiment was implemented using z-Tree software [22]. The session lasted about 40 minutes. Data were collected individually, i.e. each participant was instructed and participated in the experiment individually. In addition, there was neither practice trials nor time pressure. In particular

---

[2] It is straightforward to see that when V_0 is higher than I_2, the sure P_1 tends to be almost equal to the discounted expected value of the risky payment (P_2). In fact, the higher the underlying value compared to the exercise price, the higher the probability to exercise the call option. In such a case, the sure payment (P_1)

and the discounted expected value of the risky payment are assumed to be almost the same value.

subjects were provided with the following instructions describing the task and the interface of the computer program that was used to administer the experiment (Fig. 4).

B. Instructions

Welcome! You are about to participate in an experiment in the economics of decision-making. If you listen carefully and make good decisions, you could earn a considerable amount of money that will be paid to you in cash at the end of the experiment. The rules for the experiment are as follows. Do not talk or communicate with other participants. Do not attempt to use the computer for any other purpose than what is explicitly required by the experiment. This means you are not allowed to browse the internet, check emails, etc. If you violate any of these rules, you will be asked to leave without pay. Feel free to ask questions by raising your hand or signaling to the experimenter. During the experiment your entire earnings will be calculated in points. At the end of the experiment the total amount of points you have earned will be converted to dollars at the following rate:

(Some points)=1$

You are in control of a company that is working on a risky R&D (research and development) project with potential significant profit. A large firm that specializes in taking these kinds of projects to the final market will offer to form an alliance with you that will make your profit higher. Specifically, the large company will offer you two different kinds of contracts: a sure contract and an uncertain one.

Consequentially, you could receive a certain payoff or a payoff with uncertain outcome, which could be higher or lower than the certain one. Your **TASK** in this game is to choose between a **certain** payoff and a payoff with **uncertain** outcome. You will be shown both the amount of the certain payoff and the distribution of possible outcomes for the uncertain payoff before being asked to make a decision. The sequence of the game is as follows. At the beginning of each round, the large firm will offer you an alliance contract. You may use to accept this payoff: in which case the round will conclude. However, you may also choose to forgo the guaranteed payoff, and instead take a payoff tied to the value of your project.

Because the development of the project is risky, its value changes random. As a consequence, the alliance contract offered by the large firm – and hence your payoff - changes randomly. This means that it might go higher than the certain payoff, earning you more points. It is also possible that the payoff will be lower, earning you less points. If you choose this option, you will take a payoff randomly picked up from a given distribution, which is shown to you on the screen. You will be playing several rounds of this game, but your decision in a given round **does NOT** affect any other round.

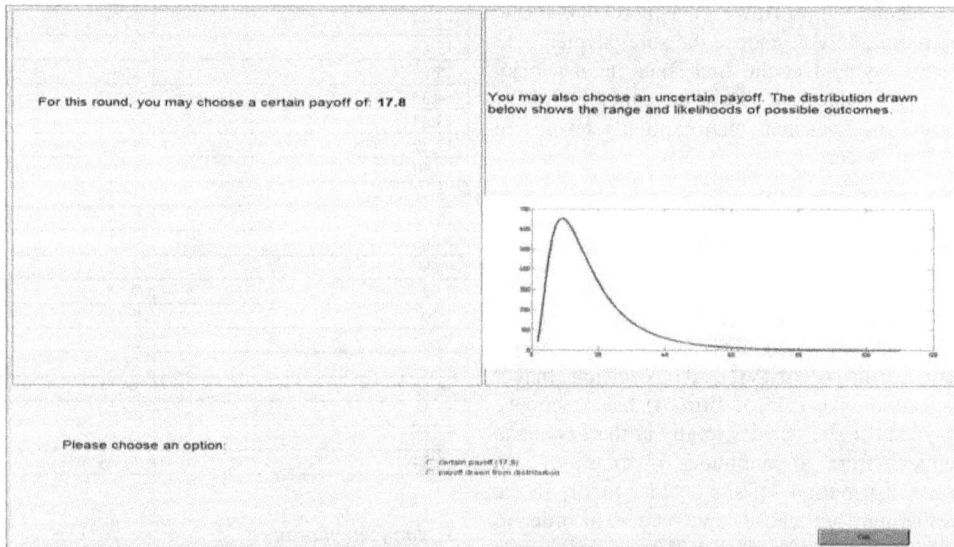

For this round, you may choose a certain payoff of: **17.8**

You may also choose an uncertain payoff. The distribution drawn below shows the range and likelihoods of possible outcomes.

Please choose an option:
○ certain payoff (17.8)
○ payoff drawn from distribution

Fig. 4. Screenshot shown during the experimental game

C. Results

Fig. 5 graphs the proportion of subjects who chose to accept the certain payment and the risky payment. Except for rounds (1-14-15-16-19) where most subjects preferred the certain payment, and for rounds (7-17-18) where the number of subjects who choose the certain payment and the risky one was the same, a large proportion of people preferred the risky payment over the other rounds (or alternately they preferred solving the uncertainty and signing the alliance at the second stage).

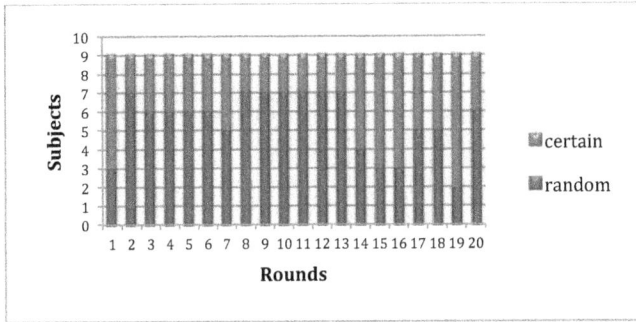

Fig. 5. Number of subjects who chose the certain payment or the random payment over the 20 rounds.

We can imagine that, given higher values of P_1 *ceteris paribus* (so that the equilibrium would be to sign the alliance at the first stage), subjects would have preferred taking the risky payment and signing the alliance at the second stage, deviating from the optimal time suggested by the normative model. Therefore, as anticipated in the introduction, risk preferences people do influence important investment decisions under uncertainty, also in the context of R&D alliances. Moreover, while evidence suggests that, when dealing with risky alternatives with gains as possible outcomes people appear risk averse, our very preliminary results do not seem confirm this result. The intuition behind is that people could make different decisions when they face with outcomes continuously distributed.

V. CONCLUSIONS AND FURTHER DEVELOPMENTS

There is a growing awareness that a large proportion of acquisition strategies fail to deliver the expected value. Too often managers make risky investments decisions based on their intuition or on their cognitive biases – such as risk aversion – exposing their companies to potentially costly pitfalls [23]. This important consideration calls for integrating mathematical models used to evaluate investments under uncertainty (i.e. real option models) with experimental economics methods in order to predict and explain the decision process, preferences and cognitive limitations that the real decision makers exhibit when deliberating over complex options.

Starting from a real options model dealing with alliance timing decisions, we propose a simple design that can been used to test some of the fundamental insights of real options theory in the context of R&D alliances. With this aim, we conducted a preliminary pilot that illustrates how the suggested design could be implemented. Of course, to effectively test the theoretical model, several rounds of the game should be played by a larger number of subjects.

There are several directions to build upon this work for future research. First, a comprehensive work should include the more complex duopoly case (please refer to Lo Nigro et al. [8]), in which people should make decisions regarding the optimal time considering not only uncertainty on the project value due to the nature of the setup (such that in the monopoly case), but also uncertainty about reactions of competitors. How does the presence of competition influence people decisions? For instance, it is recognized in option pricing literature that, in absence of competition, an incumbent firm would delay project initiation. Conversely, *ceteris paribus*, the presence of competition may speed up a firm's planned investment [24]. Under particular values of the input parameters, we find the same situation in the alliance timing problem under uncertainty (see Fig. 6). In fact, given the same input parameters, the optimal time to sign the alliance is the second stage when the monopoly case is considered, whereas it is the first stage when the duopoly case is considered.

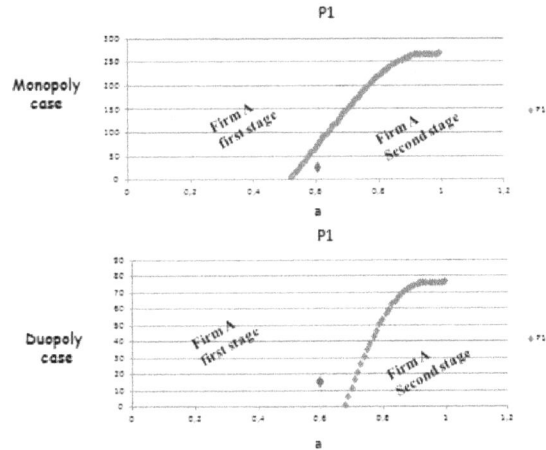

Fig. 6. P_1 Threshold when $E(P_2)$ is high (monopoly and duopoly case)

Given the same payments conditions in the duopoly structure, does the first mover anticipate the alliance at the first stage in order to pre-empt the follower? It would be very interesting to study what it can happen empirically in such a situation.

Second, our study builds also on an active literature of risk choice and individuals' risk preference [25,26]. More recent writings include Miller and Shapira [2] and Andreoni [27]). In these studies, risky choices involve probabilistic and discrete outcomes. Since we use the well known Black and Sholes formula (which assumes that the distribution of possible stock price at the end of any finite interval is lognormal), our first goal is to study individuals' risk attitudes when facing a choice between a sure outcome and a risk alternative coming from a continuous probability distribution. To the best of our knowledge, no previous works have considered risky outcomes as continuously distributed. Therefore it would be interesting to compare this continuous distribution (i.e. many outcomes) with simple binary lotteries with the same mean and variance. Based on the preliminary results of this research, we contend that people could make different decisions in front of the same risky problem. If it is the case, researchers should put attention also on the particular model used to evaluate risky investments.

ACKNOWLEDGMENTS

We are grateful to Daniel Friedman for the valuable and insightful comments and suggestions and for pilot funding. We also thank seminar participants at USCS for helpful comments.

REFERENCES

[1] T. Copeland, V. Antikarov, Real Options – A Practioner's Guide, New York: Texere, 2001.

[2] K. Miller, and Z. Shapira, ,"An Empirical Test of Heuristics and Biases Affecting Real Option Valuation," Strategic Management Journal, 2004 vol 25, pp. 269–284.

[3] AK. Dixit, and RS. Pindyck, Investment under Uncertainty. Princeton University Press: Princeton, NJ, 1994.

[4] T. Chi, "Option to Acquire and Divest a Joint Venture," Strategic Management Journal, vol 21, pp. 665-687.

[5] N. Savva, Real Options: Competition in Market Regulation and Cooperation in Partnership Deals, Phd. Dissertation, Fitzwilliam College, University of Cambridge, 2006.

[6] E. Lukas, "Dynamic market entry and the value of flexibility in transitional joint ventures," Review of Financial economics, 2007, vol 16, pp 91-110.

[7] E. Lukas, " Modeling sequential international R&D alliances under uncertainty", 2008 GEABA Discussion Paper No. 08-34.

[8] G. Lo Nigro, A. Morreale, S. Robba, P. Roma, "Biopharmaceutical Alliances and Competition: a real options games approach," International Journal of Innovation Management, 2013 vol 17 (6).

[9] K. Nischide, Y., Tian, "Compensation measures for alliance formation: A real options analysis". Economic Modelling, 2011, vol 28, pp. 219-228.

[10] R.O. Murphy, and S.D. Knaus, "Real options in the laboratory: an experimental study of sequential investment decisions, " Academy of Management Proceedings, 2011.

[11] H.T.J Smit,. and L. Trigeorgis, Strategic Investment: Real Options and Games. Princeton University Press: Princeton NJ, 2004

[12] U. Malmendier, G. Tate, "CEO overconfidence and corporate investment," Journal of Finance., 2005, vol 60, pp. 2661-2700.

[13] H.T.J Smit, and D. Lovallo, "Creating More Accurate Acquisition Valuations," MIT Sloan Management Review, 2014, vol 56, pp. 63-72.

[14] A. Yavas, and C. Sirmans, "Real Options: Experimental Evidence," The Journal of Real Estate Finance and Economics, 2005, vol 31, pp. 27–52.

[15] A. Schram, "Artificiality: The Tension Between Internal and External Validity in Economic Experiments," Journal of Economic Methodology, 2005, vol 12, pp. 225-237.

[16] S.D. Levitt, A. and J.A. List, "What Do Laboratory Experiments Measuring Social Preferences Reveal About the Real World?," Journal of Economic Perspectives, 2007, vol 21, pp. 153–74.

[17] A. Moel, and P. Tufano, "When are real options exercised? An empirical study of mine closings,". Review of Financial Studies, 2002, vol 15, pp. 35-64.

[18] R. Oprea, D. Friedman, and S. Anderson, "Learning to Wait: A Laboratory Investigation," Review of Economic Studies, 2009, vol 76, pp. 1103–24.

[19] F. Black, and M. Scholes, "The pricing of options and corporate liabilities," Journal of Political Economy, 1973, vol 81, pp. 637–654.

[20] D. Kahneman, and A. Tversky, " Choice, values, and frames," American Psychologist, 1984, vol 39, pp. 341-350.

[21] Z. Shapira, Risk Taking: A Managerial Perspective. Russell Stage Foundation: New York, 1995.

[22] U. Fischbacher, "Z-Tree: Zurich Toolbox for Ready-Made Economic Experiments," Experimental Economics, 2007, vol 10, pp. 171-178.

[23] H.T.J Smit, and T. Moraitis, Playing at Acquisitions: Behavioral Option games. Princeton University Press, 2015.

[24] M. E. Boyer, and Gravel, P. Lasserre, Real Options and Strategic Competition: A Survey. Working paper, Department of Economics and CIRANO, University of Montreal, 2004.

[25] J. Von Neumann, and O. Morgenstern, Theory of games and economic behavior (Princeton University Press, Princeton, N J), 1944.

[26] K. Arrow, Aspects of the theory of risk-taking, Yr~o Jahnsson lectures (Yr~o Jahnsson Saatio, Helsmki), 1965.

[27] J. Andreoni, and C. Sprenger, "Risk Preferences Are Not Time Preferences," American Economic Review, 2012, vol 102, pp. 3357-3376.

Real Option Values and Financial Ratios in the Finnish Stock Market

Jani Kinnunen

Institute for Advanced Management Systems Research,
Åbo Akademi University, Turku, Finland
jani.kinnunen@abo.fi

Irina Georgescu

Department of Economic Cybernetics,
Academy of Economic Sciences, Bucharest, Romania
Irina.georgescu@csie.ase.ro

Abstract— This paper studies real option values (ROVs) and financial ratios of Finnish stock-exchange listed companies using yearly financial data, i.e., financial statements and market valuations from Talouselämä database. The analysis is based on several clustering analysis methods to find out which financial ratios are linked to different levels of ROVs. We have selected the financial inputs in such a way that they include the key drivers of companies' market values above their fundamental book values to get a proxy for their real options values. We interpret the clustering results and argue that the method is applicable and valuable both for general descriptive purposes also for various market actors, such as private investors, venture capitalists and corporate acquirers in their decision making related to their target's or portfolio elements' upside potential. We find many interesting future research opportunities on real options perspective.

Keywords—Real option value, financial ratio analysis, clustering